Essential Chinese for Travel

Fan Zhilong

China Books & Periodicals, Inc.

© 1988, 1990
Revised Edition: © 1996   Second Printing 2000

ISBN: 0-8351-2575-0
Library of Congress: 96-83341

Printed in Hong Kong by Regent Publishing Services, Ltd.

CHINA
BOOKS
& Periodicals, Inc.

Contents

Publisher Acknowledgments

The publisher would like to thank the following people for their contributions to this phrasebook and tape set:

Ma Baolin for editorial.

Xu Wei, Zeng Li Zhang, and Nicolette Noyes Houseman who were the voices on the audio tape that accompanies this book.

Godwin Chu for proofreading.

Wendy K. Lee for cover and book design.

China Books & Periodicals, Inc.

Introduction

In recent years, the number of foreign tourists to China has been steadily increasing. The study of Chinese, as a result, has gained popularity throughout the world. Since its publication in 1988, *Essential Chinese for Travelers* has been one of the best-sellers among the many language books distributed by China Books & Periodicals, Inc. Thousands of copies have been sold in the United States alone. Indeed, it is one of the best phrase books available on the market. However, during the seven years since it was first published, great changes have taken place in China. Therefore it is necessary to revise the original book so that readers are not misled by some of the outdated words and phrases.

Like the original, the revised edition includes more than 2,000 handy words and phrases that will be useful in almost any situation one might encounter during a trip to China. On the street, in the hotel, at a store service desk, one can look up the necessary word in any one of the sections into which this phrase book is divided. And, if the pronunciation seems difficult, one need only point to the Chinese written character in order to communicate with a non-English speaking person.

The phrase book is arranged with the English word or phrase in the first column, followed by the official *pinyin* romanization, the English pronunciation guide and the Chinese character.

The pronunciation of the *pinyin* system follows the established Mandarin dialect, known as *"putonghua,"* which literally means "the common language." This common language is now used throughout China as the official dialect, and though based on one of the northern Chinese dialects, it is today the most widely understood form of Chinese.

At the beginning of the book is a basic instruction on the use of the Chinese pronunciation system, grammar and characters so that tourists can experiment with putting together sentences and phrases of their own.

The phrase book includes everyday expressions and names for objects–a range of words and phrases for basic communication, from getting a taxi to sending a telegram. Also provided is a handy list of useful addresses and phone numbers and a mini dictionary of all the important words that appear in the book.

There is also a section of business phrases for those who are on business trips to China. Allied to this are the banking, money, and measurement terms so necessary for business talks. And, of course, for an emergency there are terms for communicating with a doctor, nurse, or druggist.

The author of this books, Fan Zhilong, was one of the senior editors of *China Today* (formerly known as *China Reconstructs*). The monthly magazine has been published in Beijing, China, for some 40 years. One of its most popular column is called "Language Corner," which presents a continuing self-study course for beginners in learning Chinese.

About the Chinese Language

The Chinese language has a written history of over 3,000 years. Today it is spoken by more than one-fifth of the world's population. Although the complicated characters make the mastery of written Chinese a difficult academic endeavor, oral Chinese is relatively easy to learn.

What is commonly referred to as Chinese is in fact the language of the Han nationality, the largest ethnic group that makes up over 90 percent of China's total population. Despite its unified written form, the pronunciation differs greatly from one area to another, which makes communication between people from different regions difficult, if not impossible. This long standing problem has prompted the Chinese government to actively promote a standard language throughout the country for the past few decades. This standard language, known as *putonghua*, or Mandarin in the West, is now taught in all Chinese schools.

Today *putonghua* is understood by almost all Chinese, including those who can speak only their local dialects. It is also the language taught in most foreign schools as a second language. Since the 1950s, a romanized phonetic system has been adopted as part of the effort to promote the standard language. This system, known as *pinyin*, has made it possible for English speakers to pick up Chinese pronunciation easily, for most of the letters in *pinyin* have the same sound values as in English, with only a few exceptions. For example, 你好 is the Chinese for "How are you." Without a romanized phonetic system, non-Chinese speakers possibly wouldn't know how to pronounce the words. With the *pinyin* system, in which *nǐ hǎo* stands for 你好, English speakers can pronounce the words even without the help of a teacher. The tone marks on top of the vowels indicate the tone of the words, but they don't change the sound values of the letters. We will discuss tone marks later in the chapter in greater detail.

Pinyin — The Chinese Phonetic System

The study of *pinyin* is the very first step towards the mastery of *putonghua* by non-Chinese speakers. Speaking of *pinyin*, it should be noted that all Chinese characters consist of a single syllable. Most of them start with a consonant and end with a vowel or vowel combination. A few characters consist of vowels only. But none of them end with a consonant unless it is a nasal sound.

There are 23 consonants and 6 basic vowels in *pinyin*. Basic vowels can form vowel combinations with each other or with a nasal consonant. Most consonants in *pinyin* have the same pronunciation as in English. For example, "b" is pronuounced as in "boy", and "t" is pronounced as in "today". There are a few consonants with uniquely Chinese pronunciation such as q, c, zh, ch, sh, z and c. There will be more detailed explanations of them later in the chapter.

The following is a list of consonants and vowels in Chinese *pinyin:*

Consonants

pinyin	English Pronunciation	Key Words
b	bo	boy
p	po	port
m	mo	mock
f	fo	fought
d	de	deck
t	te	touch
n	ne	neck
l	le	led
g	ge	gay
k	ke	kay
h	he	hate
j	jee	jeep
q	chee	cheap
x	shee	she
zh	jr	judge
ch	tr	tree
sh	sh	shake

pinyin	English Pronunciation	Key Words
r	r	run
z	ds	words
c	ts	boats
s	s	son
y	y	yes
w	w	we

Single Vowels

a	a	father
o	aw	awe
e	eh	her
i	ee	bee
u	oo	boot
ü	as the French "tu" or German "fuhlen."	Try a long "ee" with rounded lips.

Vowel Combinations

er	er	purse
ai	-ye	eye
ei	ay	bay
ao	ow	now

pinyin	English Pronunciation	Key Words
ou	o	go
an	an	can
en	en	bend
ang	ong	gown
eng	eng	sung
ong	ong	kong
ia	ia	Malaysia
ie	ie	yes
iao	iao	yowl
iu	iou	you
ian	ien	yen
in	in	gin
iang	iang	young
ing	ing	sing
iong	iung	German "junger"
ua	ua	guano
uo	uo	wall
uai	why	why
ui	we	we
uan	one	one
un	wen	went
uang	uang	oo + ang

pinyin	English Pronunciation	Key Words
üe	yue	ü +eh
üan	yuan	ü +an
ün	yun	ü +in

Difficult Point of *Pinyin* System

1. Consonants with pronunciation different from English:

Q sounds like chee in cheap, cheer, chin;

X sounds like shee in show, she, shine;

ZH is between "dr" in drive and "j" in judge. The combination "jr" is the closest one can get;

CH sounds like tr in tree, tractor, transfer;

Z sounds like ds in words, records, birds;

C sounds like ts in cats, dots, products;

R sounds like ur in pleasure and leisure.

The above sounds are uniquely Chinese and are the most difficult for non-Chinese speakers to learn. However, with some patience and the equivalent English pronunciation, learners should be able to find at least the aproximate sound.

2. The pronunciation of "i". Under normal situations, "i" sounds like ee. For example:

Pinyin	English pronunciation	English translation	Chinese characters
xuéxí	shueh shee	study	学习
rìjì	rrr gee	diary	日记
píqì	pee chee	temper	脾气
yìqǐ	yee chee	together	一起

However, when "i" appears after consonants zh, ch, shi, z, c, s, and r, it is not pronounced. Here its main function is to make the syllable complete and to prolong the sound of the consonants. For example, *zhi* would sound like drrr..., *zi* like dzzz..., and *si* like sss... See the following examples:

Pinyin	English pronunciation	English translation	Chinese characters
zhīshi	jrr shrr	knowledge	知识
rìzi	rrr dzz	living (a life)	日子
chǐzi	chr dzz	ruler	尺子
sìcì	sse tss	four times	四次

3. Tone and Tone Marks

The Chinese language has different tones that are capable of differentiating meanings. Differences in tone convey different meanings to otherwise identical or similar syllables. In the Beijing dialect, which Mandarin Chinese is based on, there are four basic tones. Using the syllable "*ba*" as an example, they are as follow:

First tone: represented by the tone-graph " ¯ ": a high, level pitch. *Bā* (八) in this tone can mean the number "8."

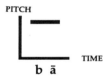

Second tone: represented by the tone-graph " ´ ": a rising tone, starting about mid-range of a speaker's voice, and ending slightly above the first tone. *Bá* (拔) can mean "to uproot."

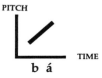

Third tone: represented by the tone-graph " ˇ ": a dipping pitch, falling from mid-range to low, then rising. *Bǎ* (把) can mean "to hold".

PITCH

TIME

b ǎ

Fourth tone: represented by the tone-graph " ` ": a sharply falling pitch, starting near the top of the speaker's range and reaching mid-to-low-level at the end. *Bà* (霸) can mean "tyrant" or "despot."

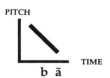

PITCH

TIME

b ā

In addition, brief, unstressed syllables may also occur and take a feeble tone, such as *ba* (吧). They have no tone mark.

Chinese Characters — A Pictographic Language

Chinese characters are the symbols used in written Chinese. Modern Chinese charaters fall into two categories: those with a phonetic component and those without it. Most of the characters without a phonetic component have developed from pictographs. From ancient writings on archaelogical relics we can see their evolution:

⊙	⊖	⊟	日	*rì*	sun
☽	D	☽	月	*yuè*	moon
⺈	⼅	儿	人	*rén*	person
大	米	朮	木	*mù*	tree

The above examples represent specific objects, of which it is easy to draw a picture. For those words that represent abstract concepts, their original symbols tell of the imagination of the Chinese people. See the following examples on the Chinese characters for "up" and "down."

⌣	⊥	⼂	上	*rén*	person
⌢	⊤	⼂	下	*mù*	tree

It is easy to tell the meaning of 上 (*shàng*) and 下 (*xià*) from the characters. Putting the two words together, the Chinese have made a new word 卡 (*kǎ*), which means "stuck in the middle."

The combination of two or more simple characters very often results in a new word. This is a very common way in which many Chinese characters are created. The meaning of the new words can normally be explained from the original words. For example:

日 (*rì*), the sun, and 月 (*yuè*), the moon = 明 (*míng*), meaning bright or light;

人 (*rén*), a person, and 木 (*mù*), a tree = 休 (*xiū*), meaning having a rest (this word features a man leaning against a tree);

木 (*mù*), a tree, and 木 (*mù*), a tree = 林 (lín), meaning forest.

The fact that many commonly used Chinese words can trace their origins to such meaningful combinations makes the study of Chinese characters much more interesting. It also makes the Chinese language less intimidating for non-Chinese speakers to learn. After all, writing Chinese characters is not as complicated as drawing a picture.

The Structure of Words and Rules of Wrting

Chinese characters may look very complicated. Some of them are so indeed. However, the writing of Chinese characters could be made easy if the basic strokes are learned. And the basic strokes, as shown below, are rather simple and easy to learn.

Stroke	Name		
、	点	*dián*	dot
一	横	*héng*	horizontal
丨	竖	*shù*	vertical
丿	撇	*piě*	left-falling
乀	捺	*nà*	right-falling
丿	提	*tí*	rising
亅乚乀	钩	*gōu*	hook
乛一	折	*zhé*	turning

These strokes are basically straight lines and should not be written in curls like English letters. All of them are written from top to bottom and from left to right, with the exception of tí, the rising stroke. Please note the arrows as they indicate how the strokes are written:

After learning the strokes, one is ready to learn to write the characters. Chinese characters are generally composed of two or more basic structural parts known as "character component." Some components can stand by themselves with full meaning. For example, 人 *(rén)* is a character itself. It can also be a character component in other words, such as in 休 *(xiu)*.

For those words that have two or more components, some are made up of upper and lower parts, some of left and right, others of inside and outside. The writing of Chinese words follows some basic rules in terms of stroke order (i.e.: from top to bottom and from left to right). When a word is composed of an inside and outside part, such as 国 *(guó,* country), always start with the outside, but finish the inside part before closing the box. The following examples show the basic rule of stroke order:

Example	Stroke Order	Rule
十	一　十	First Horizontal, then vertical
人	ノ　人	First left-falling, then right-falling
三	一　二　三	From top to bottom
州	丶　丿　丬　州　州　州	From left to right
月	丿　刀　月　月	First outside then inside
四	丨　冂　冋　四　四	Finish inside, then close
小	丨　小　小	Middle, then the two sides

Adjectives and Adverbs

In English, a sentence is incomplete without a verb. For example, "you good" is grammatically incorrect, as is "the clothes beautiful." To make these sentences complete and correct, the verb "be" must be added. In Chinese, however, the word "be", or 是 (shì), would be redundant if it appears in-between a subject and an adjective. For instance, 你好 (nǐ hǎo) is a complete sentence itself. The verb 是 is not needed. Instead, the Chinese would, in many cases, add the word 很 (hěn), or "very," in front the adjectives. Following are some commonly used adjectives:

Pinyin	English pronunciation	English translation	Chinese characters
hǎo	how	good	好
máng	mang	busy	忙
guì	gwei	expensive	贵
piányi	pien yee	cheap	便宜
duō	dwo	many	多
shǎo	shao	few	少
dà	dah	big	大
xiǎo	shiao	small	小

Following are some commonly used nouns and pronouns. You can try to use them together with the adjectives above. Remember, you can always add the word 很 *(hěn)*, or "very", in-between the subject and the adjective.

Pinyin	English pronunciation	English translation	Chinese characters
wǒ	wo	I	我
nǐ	nee	you	你
tā	tah	he	他
zhèigè	jray geh	this one	这个
nèigè	nay geh	that one	那个

If you haven't figured out how to use these words together, here is an example:

Pinyin	English pronunciation	English translation	Chinese
wǒ hěn máng	wo hen mang	I (am) very busy.	我很忙。

You can also leave out the word 很 *(hěn)* by simply saying 我忙 *(wǒ máng)* or "I (am) busy."

Present, Past and Future Tense

Chinese verbs are easy to use because they don't change with the time of the action. Verbs remain in the same form whether they represent present, past or future actions. The difference in time is indicated with a time word such as "today" (今天 *jīntiān*) or "tomorrow" (明天 *míngtiān*). It can also be known through words like 了 *(le)* or 过 *(guò)*, both of which indicate that the action is already completed.

For example, in the sentence 我去中国 (*wǒ qù Zhōngguó*), "I go to China," the verb 去 *(qù)* remains the same no matter when the action takes place. One can use additional words to indicate the time of action.

English translation	Pinyin/Pronunciation	Chinese
He goes to China.	*tā qù Zhōngguó* tah chu jrong gwo	他去中国。
He will go to China tomorrow.	*tā <u>míngtiān</u> qù Zhōngguó* tah ming tien chu jrong gwo	他明天去中国。

He went to China yesterday.   他昨天去中国了。
tā zuótiān qù Zhōngguó le
tah dzwo tien chu jrong gwo le

He has been to China (before).   他去过中国。
tā qù guò Zhōngguó
tah chu gwo jrong gwo

He has gone to China (he is still there).   他去中国了。
tā qù Zhōngguó le
tah chu jrong gwo le

Everyday Terms and Phrases

This section lists some of the most frequently used words, phrases, and simple sentences. Words and phrases are arranged in alphabetical order. Sentences are arranged in order of content. All entries begin with the English term, followed by *pinyin*, a pronunciation guide, and Chinese characters.

The section is divided into the following categories:

Most Frequently Used Words and Phrases;
Questions;
Antonyms;
Numbers;
Time;
Days, Months and Seasons;
Holidays and Festivals;
Weather;
Measure Words and Quantities.

This categorization is intended to make it easy for the readers to find the words relevant to the situation.

English translation	*Pinyin*	Pronunciation	Chinese

Most Frequently Used Words and Phrases

English translation	*Pinyin*	Pronunciation	Chinese
also	*yě*	yeh	也
at/in/on	*zài*	dzai	在
buy	*mǎi*	my	买
come	*lái*	lie	来
drink	*hē*	huh	喝
eat	*chī*	chir	吃
from	*cóng*	tsung	从
get off (bus)	*xià (chē)*	shiah (chuh)	下（车）
get on (bus)	*shàng (chē)*	shang (chuh)	上（车）
give	*gěi*	gay	给
go	*qù*	chu	去
have	*yǒu*	you	有
learn/study	*xuéxí*	shueh shee	学习
like/dislike	*xǐhuān/bù xǐhuān*	shee huan/boo shee huan	喜欢、不喜欢
listen	*tīng*	ting	听
lose (game)	*shū*	shoo	输
lose (object)	*diū*	dew	丢
or	*háishì/huòzhě*	high shir/hwo jre	还是、或者
perhaps	*yěxǔ*	yeh shu	也许

English translation	*Pinyin*	Pronunciation	Chinese
read	*dú*	doo	读
rest	*xiūxi*	show shee	休息
see/look	*kàn*	can	看
sell	*mài*	my	卖
sleep	*shuìjiào*	shui jiao	睡觉
soon	*bùjiǔ*	boo geo	不久
speak	*shuō*	shuo	说
toward	*xiàng*	shiang	向
very	*fēicháng*	fay chang	非常
walk	*zǒulù*	dzoh loo	走路
want	*yào*	yaw	要
write	*xiě*	shieh	写
I don't know.	*wǒ bù zhīdào*	wo boo jrr daw	我不知道。
I am not sure.	*wǒ bù qīngchu*	wo boo ching chu	我不清楚。
I understand.	*wǒ míngbai*	wo ming bye	我明白。
I don't understand.	*wǒ bù míngbai*	wo boo ming bye	我不明白。

Questions

how long (time)	*duō jiǔ*	duo geo	多久
how big	*duō dà*	duo dah	多大

English translation	Pinyin	Pronunciation	Chinese
how far	*duō yuǎn*	duo yuan	多远
how much/how many	*duōshǎo*	duo shaw	多少
what	*shénme*	shen ma	什么
when	*shénme shíhòu*	shen ma shir hoh	什么时候
where	*nǎlǐ, nǎr*	na lee, na er	哪里、哪儿
which one	*nǎ yī gè*	na yee geh	哪一个
who	*shuí*	shay	谁
why	*wèi shénme*	way shen ma	为什么
How much does it cost?	*duōshǎo qián*	duo shaw chien	多少钱？
What is this?	*zhè shì shénme*	jre shir shen ma	这是什么？
What time is it?	*xiànzài jǐ diǎn zhōng*	shien dzai gee dien drung	现在几点钟？
What does this mean?	*zhè shì shénme yìsi*	jre shir shen ma yee sse	这是什么意思？
What did you say?	*nǐ shuō shénme*	nee shuo shen ma	你说什么？
What's the matter?	*zěnme huí shì*	dzen ma hui shir	怎么回事？
Where are we?	*zhè shì shénme dìfāng*	jre shir shen ma dee fang	这是什么地方？
When will it be ready?	*shénme shíhòu néng hǎo*	shen ma shir hoh neng how	什么时候能好？
Do you speak English?	*nǐ shuō yīngyǔ ma*	nee shuo ying yu ma	你说英语吗？

English translation	Pinyin	Pronunciation	Chinese
French	*fǎyǔ*	fah yu	法语
German	*déyǔ*	deh yu	德语
Spanish	*xībānyáyǔ*	shee ban yah yu	西班牙语
Japanese	*rìyǔ*	rrr yu	日语

Antonyms

beautiful/ugly	*měi/chǒu*	may/chow	美、丑
before/now/after	*yǐqián/xiànzài/yǐhòu*	yee chien/shien dzai/yee hoh	以前、现在、以后
beneath/above	*xiàbiān/shàngbiān*	shiah bien/shang bien	下边、上边
big/small	*dà/xiǎo*	dah/shiao	大、小
bright/dark	*míngliàng/huīàn*	ming liang/hui an	明亮、灰暗
cheap/expensive	*piányi/guì*	pien yee/gwe	便宜、贵
clean/dirty	*gānjìng/zāng*	gang gin/dzang	干净、脏
deep/shallow	*shēn/qiǎn*	shen/chien	深、浅
dry/wet	*gān/shī*	gun/shir	干、湿
early/late	*zǎo/wǎn*	dzao/wan	早、晚
easy/difficult	*róngyi/nán*	rung yee/nan	容易、难
fat/thin	*pàng/shòu*	pong/show	胖、瘦
first/last	*xiān/hòu*	shien/hoh	先、后

English translation	Pinyin	Pronunciation	Chinese
front/back	*qián/hòu*	chien/hoh	前、后
full/empty	*mǎn/kōng*	man/koong	满、空
good/bad	*hǎo/huài*	how/hwai	好、坏
happy/sad	*gāoxìng/bēi'āi*	gao shing/bay eye	高兴、悲哀
heavy/light	*zhòng/qīng*	drung/chin	重、轻
here/there	*zhèlǐ/nàlǐ*	jre lee/nah lee	这里、那里
high/low	*gāo/dī*	gao/dee	高、低
hot/cold	*rè/lěng*	re/leng	热、冷
hungry/full	*è/bǎo*	uh/bow	饿、饱
inside/outside	*lǐbiān/wàibiān*	lee bien/why bien	里边、外边
interesting/boring	*yǒu yìsi/méi jìn*	you yee sse/may gin	有意思、没劲
left/right	*zuǒ/yòu*	dzuo/you	左、右
long/short	*cháng/duǎn*	chang/dwan	长、短
many/few	*duō/shǎo*	dwo/shao	多、少
narrow/wide	*zhǎi/kuān*	jrai/kwan	窄、宽
near/far	*jìn/yuǎn*	gin/yuan	近、远
old/new	*jiù/xīn*	geo/shin	旧、新
old/young	*lǎo/shào*	lao/shao	老、少
open/close	*kāi/guān*	kai/gwan	开、关
ordinary/peculiar	*pǔtōng/qíguài*	poo tung/chee gwai	普通、奇怪
quick/slow	*kuài/màn*	kwai/man	快、慢

English translation	*Pinyin*	Pronunciation	Chinese
quiet/noisy	*ānjìng/chǎonào*	an gin/chaw naw	安静、吵闹
rich/poor	*fù/qióng*	foo/chiung	富、穷
right/wrong	*duì/cuò*	dwei/tsuo	对、错
safe/dangerous	*ānquán/wēixiǎn*	an chuan/way shian	安全、危险
simple/complex	*jiǎndān/fùzá*	jien dan/foo dzah	简单、复杂
smart/stupid	*cōngming/yúchǔn*	tsung ming/yu chun	聪明、愚蠢
soft/hard	*ruǎn/yìng*	ruan/ying	软、硬
strong/weak	*qiángzhuàng/ ruǎnruò*	chiang drung/ ruan raw	强壮、软弱
tall/short	*gāo/ǎi*	gao/eye	高、矮
true/false	*zhēn/jiǎ*	jren/jiah	真、假

Numbers

number	*shùzì, hàomǎ*	shu dze, how mah	数字、号码
zero	*líng*	ling	零
one	*yī*	yee	一
two	*èr*	er	二
three	*sān*	son	三
four	*sì*	sse	四
five	*wǔ*	woo	五

English translation	Pinyin	Pronunciation	Chinese
six	*liù*	lew	六
seven	*qī*	chee	七
eight	*bā*	bah	八
nine	*jiǔ*	geo	九
ten	*shí*	shir	十
eleven	*shíyī*	shir yee	十一
twelve	*shí'èr*	shir er	十二
thirteen	*shísān*	shir son	十三
fourteen	*shísì*	shir sse	十四
fifteen	*shíwǔ*	shir woo	十五
sixteen	*shíliù*	shir lew	十六
seventeen	*shíqī*	shir chee	十七
eighteen	*shíbā*	shir bah	十八
nineteen	*shíjiǔ*	shir geo	十九
twenty	*èrshí*	er shir	二十
twenty-one	*èrshíyī*	er shir yee	二十一
twenty-five	*èrshíwǔ*	er shir woo	二十五
thirty	*sānshí*	son shir	三十
thirty-three	*sānshísān*	son shir son	三十三
forty	*sìshí*	sse shir	四十
fifty	*wǔshí*	woo shir	五十

English translation	*Pinyin*	Pronunciation	Chinese
sixty	*liùshí*	lew shir	六十
seventy	*qīshí*	chee shir	七十
eighty	*bāshí*	bah shir	八十
ninety	*jiǔshí*	geo shir	九十
one hundred	*yìbǎi*	yee bye	一百
one hundred ten	*yìbǎiyīshí*	yee bye yee shir	一百一十
two hundred	*èrbǎi*	er bye	二百
three hundred	*sānbǎi*	son bye	三百
four hundred	*sìbǎi*	sse bye	四百
five hundred	*wǔbǎi*	woo bye	五百
six hundred	*liùbǎi*	lew bye	六百
seven hundred	*qībǎi*	chee bye	七百
eight hundred	*bābǎi*	bah bye	八百
nine hundred	*jiǔbǎi*	geo bye	九百
one thousand	*yìqiān*	yee chien	一千
ten thousand	*yíwàn*	yee wan	一万
one hundred thousand	*shíwàn*	shir wan	十万
one million	*yìbǎiwàn*	yee bye wan	一百万
one hundred million	*yíyì*	yee yee	一亿

English translation	*Pinyin*	Pronunciation	Chinese
first	*dìyī*	dee yee	第一
second	*dì'èr*	dee er	第二
third	*dìsān*	dee son	第三
fourth	*dìsì*	dee sse	第四
fifth	*dìwǔ*	dee woo	第五
sixth	*dìliù*	dee lew	第六
seventh	*dìqī*	dee chee	第七
eighth	*dìbā*	dee bah	第八
ninth	*dìjiǔ*	dee geo	第九
tenth	*dìshí*	dee shir	第十

Time

English translation	*Pinyin*	Pronunciation	Chinese
early morning	*qīngzǎo*	ching dzaw	清早
morning	*shàngwǔ*	shang woo	上午
noon	*zhōngwǔ*	drung woo	中午
afternoon	*xiàwǔ*	shiah woo	下午
evening	*wǎnshàng*	wan shang	晚上
night	*yèlǐ*	yeh lee	夜里
day	*báitiān/tiān*	bye tien/tien	白天、天
week	*xīngqī*	shing chee	星期

English translation	Pinyin	Pronunciation	Chinese
month	*yuè*	yueh	月
season	*jì*	gee	季
year	*nián*	nien	年
this year	*jīnnián*	gin nien	今年
this month	*zhèige yuè*	jre geh yueh	这个月
this week	*zhèige xīngqī*	jre geh shing chee	这个星期
next year	*míngnián*	ming nien	明年
next month	*xià gè yuè*	shiah geh yueh	下个月
next week	*xià gè xīngqī*	shiah geh shing chee	下个星期
today	*jīntiān*	gin tien	今天
yesterday	*zuótiān*	dzaw tien	昨天
last night	*zuówǎn*	dzaw wan	昨晚
tomorrow	*míngtiān*	ming tien	明天
day after tomorrow	*hòutiān*	hoh tien	后天
now	*xiànzài*	shien dzai	现在
hour	*xiǎoshí*	shiao shir	小时
minute	*fēn*	fen	分
second	*miǎo*	miao	秒
half an hour	*bàn xiǎoshí*	ban shiao shir	半小时
a quarter	*yí kè zhōng*	yee keh drung	一刻钟

English translation	Pinyin	Pronunciation	Chinese
What time is it?	*xiànzài jǐ diǎn zhōng*	shien dzai gee dien drung	现在几点钟?
It is three o'clock.	*xiànzài sān diǎn zhōng*	shien dzai san dien drung	现在三点钟。
three thirty	*sān diǎn bàn*	san dien ban	三点半
ten to twelve	*shí'èr diǎn chà shí fēn*	shir er dien chah shir fen	十二点差十分
five fifteen	*wǔ diǎn yí kè*	woo dien yee keh	五点一刻

Days of the Week, Months and Seasons

Sunday	*xīngqīrì*	shing chee ri	星期日
Monday	*xīngqīyī*	shing chee yee	星期一
Tuesday	*xīngqī'èr*	shing chee er	星期二
Wednesday	*xīngqīsān*	shing chee son	星期三
Thursday	*xīngqīsì*	shing chee sse	星期四
Friday	*xīngqīwǔ*	shing chee woo	星期五
Saturday	*xīngqīliù*	shing chee lew	星期六
weekend	*zhōu mò*	jrou mo	周末
January	*yíyuè*	yee yueh	一月
February	*èryuè*	er yueh	二月

English translation	*Pinyin*	Pronunciation	Chinese
March	*sānyuè*	son yueh	三月
April	*sìyuè*	sse yueh	四月
May	*wǔyuè*	woo yueh	五月
June	*liùyuè*	lew yueh	六月
July	*qīyuè*	chee yueh	七月
August	*bāyuè*	bah yueh	八月
September	*jiǔyuè*	geo yueh	九月
October	*shíyuè*	shir yueh	十月
November	*shíyīyuè*	shir yee yueh	十一月
December	*shí'èryuè*	shir er yueh	十二月
spring	*chūntiān*	chun tien	春天
summer	*xiàtiān*	shiah tien	夏天
autumn	*qiūtiān*	chew tien	秋天
winter	*dōngtiān*	doong tien	冬天
What day is it today?	*jīntiān xīngqī jǐ*	gin tien shing chee gee	今天星期几？
It is Monday.	*jīntiān xīngqīyī*	gin tien shing chee yee	今天星期一。
What date is it today?	*jīntiān shì jǐ hào*	gin tien shir gee how	今天是几号？

English translation	Pinyin	Pronunciation	Chinese
It is January 1.	*jīntiān shì yíyuè yíhào*	gin tien shir yee yueh yee how	今天是一月一号
February 2	*èryuè èr hào*	er yueh er how	二月二号
March 10	*sānyuè shí hào*	son yueh shir how	三月十号
October 20	*shíyuè èrshí hào*	shir yueh er shir how	十月二十号

Holidays and Festivals

April Fool's Day	*yúrénjié*	yu ren jieh	愚人节
Children's Day (June 1)	*értóng jié*	er tong jieh	儿童节
Chinese New Year	*chūnjié*	chun jieh	春节
Christmas	*shèngdànjié*	shen dan jieh	圣诞节
Dragon Boat Festival	*duānwǔ jié*	dwan woo jieh	端午节
Easter	*fù huó jié*	foo hwo jieh	复活节
Mid-Autumn Festival	*zhōngqiūjié*	drung chew jieh	中秋节
National Day	*guóqìng jié*	gwo ching jieh	国庆节
New Year's Day	*xīnnián, yuándàn*	shing nien, yuan dan	新年，元旦
Qingming Festival (April 5)	*qīngmíng jié*	ching ming jieh	清明节

English translation	*Pinyin*	Pronunciation	Chinese
Thanksgiving	*gǎn'ēnjié*	gang en jieh	感恩节
Valentine's Day	*qíngrén jié*	ching ren jieh	情人节
Women's Day	*fùnǚ jié*	foo nuh jieh	妇女节

Weather

climate	*qìhòu*	chee hou	气候
cloudy	*yīn tiān*	yin tien	阴天
cold	*lěng*	leng	冷
cool	*liáng*	liang	凉
fine (weather)	*qíng tiān*	ching tien	晴天
foggy	*yǒu wù*	you woo	有雾
heavy rain	*dà yǔ*	dah yu	大雨
hot	*rè*	re	热
mild (temperature)	*bù lěng bú rè*	boo leng boo re	不冷不热
rain	*xià yǔ*	shiah yu	下雨
snow	*xià xuě*	shiah shieh	下雪
storm	*bào fēng yǔ*	baw feng yu	暴风雨
sunny	*yǒu tàiyang*	you tie yang	有太阳
temperature	*wēndù*	wen doo	温度
thunder	*léi*	lay	雷

English translation	Pinyin	Pronunciation	Chinese
typhoon	*tái fēng*	tie feng	台风
weather forecast	*tiānqì yùbào*	tien chee yu baw	天气预报
weather	*tiānqì*	tien chee	天气
windy	*yǒu fēng*	you feng	有风
How is the weather today?	*jīntiān de tiānqì zěnme yàng*	gin tien de tien chee dzen ma yang	今天的天气 怎么样？
It is a clear day.	*shì qíngtiān*	shir ching tien	是晴天
It is cool.	*hěn liángkuài*	hen liang kwai	很凉快
It is fine.	*tiānqì hěn hǎo*	tien chee hen how	天气很好
It is foggy.	*yǒu wù*	you woo	有雾
It is hot.	*tiānqì hěn rè*	tien chee hen re	天气很热
It is humid.	*tiānqì mènrè*	tien chee men re	天气闷热
It is raining.	*xià yǔ le*	shiah yu le	下雨了
It is snowing.	*xià xuě le*	shiah shieh le	下雪了
It is sunny.	*yǒu tàiyang*	you tie yang	有太阳
It is windy.	*yǒu fēng*	you feng	有风
What is the temperature today?	*jīntiān de wēndù shì duōshǎo*	gin tien de wen doo shir dwo shao	今天的温度 是多少？
How is the weather tomorrow?	*míngtiān de tiānqì zěnme yàng*	ming tien de tien chee dzen ma yang	明天的天气怎 么样？

English translation	*Pinyin*	Pronunciation	Chinese

Measure Words and Quantities

English translation	*Pinyin*	Pronunciation	Chinese
about	*chà bu duō*	chah boo duo	差不多
acre	*yīngmǔ*	ying moo	英亩
catty (500 grams)	*jīn*	gin	斤
a dozen	*yì dá*	yee dah	一打
enough	*gòu le*	go le	够了
a few	*yì xiē*	yee shieh	一些
foot (length)	*yīngchǐ*	ying chir	英尺
half	*yí bàn*	yee ban	一半
hectare	*gōngqǐng*	gong ching	公顷
inch	*yīngcùn*	ying tsun	英寸
kilogram	*gōngjīn*	goong gin	公斤
kilometer	*gōnglǐ*	goong lee	公里
many	*hěn duō*	hen daw	很多
meter	*mǐ*	mee	米
mile	*yīnglǐ*	ying lee	英里
ounce	*àngsī*	ang sse	盎司
a pair	*yí duì*	yee dui	一对
pound (weight)	*bàng*	bong	磅
percent	*bǎi fēn bǐ*	bye fen bee	百分比

English translation	Pinyin	Pronunciation	Chinese
quarter	*sì fēn zhī yī*	sse fen jrr yee	四分之一
several	*jǐ gè/yì xiē*	gee geh/yee shieh	几个、一些
whole	*zhěng gè*	jreng geh	整个

Courtesy In Conversation

As one of the oldest civilizations in the world, the Chinese culture is burdened with a rather complicated system of formalities. To understand and be able to use them all in everyday life is a difficult, if not impossible task, even for the Chinese to accomplish. As a matter fact, many young people grow up using fewer and fewer formalities and tend to be more and more casual.

However, some basic forms of courtesy still persist. For example, when two or more people go into a room, the older and/or the higher ranking person is allowed to enter first. But what if all of them are of the same age and ranking? In this situation, everyone tries to back off and let the others go in first. They would stop at the door and say: "You go first, you go first." Once a famous writer felt fed up with people asking him to go first and told his group the following story. A woman was pregnant for ten years and the baby was still not born. The doctor had no idea about the cause, so he operated on her. When he cut open her tummy, he found out that the woman had twins, both of whom insisted that the other go first.

So much for jokes. Seriously, as with other peoples, some forms of courtesy are expected in the daily communication of the Chinese people. Certainly when you ask for a favor, you are expected to say "please," (*qǐng*), rather than to act bluntly. And you should say "thank you" when you are given a favor or help.

One point that is worth mentioning here has to do with compliments. The Chinese take compliments very differently from Americans. For example, when someone says "your sweater is beautiful," Americans would say "thank you," while the typical Chinese response would be "no, it is not beautiful." For the Chinese, a negative answer to a compliment means no offense at all. On the contrary, it can't be more proper. However, certain changes have taken place in China over the past few years, partly due to the increasing amount of foreign influence. Today more and more Chinese, especially the young and educated, are adapting to the American way of saying "thank you" rather than "no" to a compliment.

It should not be surprising that people in different cultures behave differently. That is why there is the saying "when you are in Rome, do as the Romans do." In this section, you will learn words and phrases that represent the proper ways of communicating with one another. Also included is a list of professional titles that you might find useful.

English translation	*Pinyin*	Pronunciation	Chinese

Greetings and Forms of Address

good	*hǎo*	how	好
please	*qǐng*	ching	请
polite	*kèqì*	keh chee	客气
right (correct)	*duì*	dwei	对
rude	*bú kèqi*	boo keh chee	不客气
wrong	*cuò*	tswo	错

How do you do?	*nǐhǎo*	nee how	你好！
How are you?	*nǐhǎo, nǐ hǎo ma*	nee how, nee how ma	你好、你好吗？
I'm fine. Thank you.	*wǒ hěn hǎo, xiè xiè*	wo hen how, shieh shieh	我很好，谢谢。
My name is Tom.	*wǒ de míngzi jiào tāng mǔ*	wo de ming dzz jiao tang moo	我的名字叫汤姆。
What is your name?	*nǐ jiào shénme míngzi*	nee jiao shen ma ming dzz	你叫什么名字？
This is Mr. Li.	*zhè shì lǐ xiānsheng*	jre shr lee shien sheng	这是李先生。
This is Mrs. Liu.	*zhè shì liú tàitai*	jre shr lew tai tai	这是刘太太。
This is Miss Wang.	*zhè shì wáng xiǎojie*	jre shr wang shiao jieh	这是王小姐。

English translation	Pinyin	Pronunciacion	Chinese
(I'm) glad to meet you.	*hěn gāoxìng rènshi nǐ*	hen gao shing ren shr nee	很高兴认识你。
See you later.	*huí tóu jiàn*	hwei tow jien	回头见。
Good-bye	*zàijiàn*	dzai jien	再见。
Good morning.	*zǎoshàng hǎo*	dzao shang how	早上好。
Good afternoon.	*xiàwǔ hǎo, nǐhǎo*	shiah woo how, nee how	下午好、你好！
Good evening.	*wǎnshàng hǎo*	wan shang how	晚上好。
Good night	*wǎn ān*	wan an	晚安。
See you tomorrow.	*míngtiān jiàn*	ming tien jien	明天见。
Thank you.	*xièxie*	shieh shieh	谢谢。
You are welcome.	*bú yòng xiè*	boo yong shieh	不用谢。
Don't mention it.	*bú kèqi*	boo keh chee	不客气。
Please come in.	*qǐng jìn*	ching gin	请进。
Please sit down.	*qǐng zuò*	ching dzwo	请坐。
Please wait a second.	*qǐng děng yíxiàr.*	ching deng yee shiah	请等一下儿。
Excuse me.	*láo jià*	lao jia	劳驾。
I'm sorry.	*duì buqǐ*	dwei boo chee	对不起。
Could you do me a favor?	*nǐ néng bāngbang máng ma*	nee neng bang bang mang ma	你能帮帮忙吗？

English translation	Pinyin	Pronunciation	Chinese

Pronouns

English translation	Pinyin	Pronunciation	Chinese
I	*wǒ*	wo	我
you	*nǐ/nǐmen*	nee/nee men	你、你们
he	*tā*	tah	他
she	*tā*	tah	她
it	*tā*	tah	它
we	*wǒmen*	wo men	我们
they	*tāmen*	tah men	他们
my/mine	*wǒ de*	wo de	我的
your/yours	*nǐ de/nǐmen de*	nee de, nee men de	你的、你们的
his	*tā de*	tah de	他的
her/hers	*tā de*	tah de	她的
their/theirs	*tāmen de*	tah men de	他们的

Professional Titles

English translation	Pinyin	Pronunciation	Chinese
actor/actress	*nán yǎnyuán/ nǚ yǎnyuán*	nan yen yuen/ nui yen yuen	男演员、 女演员
banker	*yínháng jiā*	yin hung gia	银行家

English translation	*Pinyin*	Pronunciation	Chinese
doctor	*yīshēng*	yee sheng	医生
editor	*biānji*	bien gee	编辑
engineer	*gōngchéngshī*	gong cheng shr	工程师
farmer	*nóngmín*	nong min	农民
journalist	*jìzhě*	gee jre	记者
lawyer	*lǜshī*	lui shr	律师
musician	*yīnyuèjiā*	yin yueh gia	音乐家
nurse	*hùshi*	hoo shr	护士
photographer	*shèyǐngshī*	sheh ying shr	摄影师
professor	*jiàoshòu*	jiao shou	教授
scientist	*kēxuéjiā*	keh shueh gia	科学家
secretary	*mìshū*	mee shu	秘书
student	*xuéshēng*	shueh sheng	学生
teacher	*lǎoshī*	lao shr	老师
technician	*jìshùyuán*	gee shu yuen	技术员
translator	*fānyì*	fan yee	翻译
worker	*gōngrén*	gong ren	工人
writer	*zuòjiā*	dzwo gia	作家
tour guide	*dǎoyóu*	dao you	导游

Travel

Among the large number of tourists who visit China each year, most travel there with a tour group. The advantage of joining in a group is obvious. You don't have to worry about itinerary, ticket, visa, hotel, food, transportation, and so on. Everything is arranged for you. Therefore you can enjoy a carefree trip.

Your travel agency will arrange for a tour guide to meet you at the airport and lead you throughout your trip. Most of the tour guides are bilingual in Chinese and English. They are trained to give you introductions to the places you visit and make travel arrangements.

At the end of each day, every tourist is expected to tip the guide for one dollar. This is a drastic change from a decade ago, when tips were discouraged in all service industries in China. Today tour guides are among the richest individuals, partly because of the tips they receive from their customers. However, their main source of income is from commissions paid by the stores patronized by foreign tourists. When tour guides take a group to a store, they get a portion of the total sales. Five years ago there was a crackdown on such practices in Beijing. But nothing has really changed.

This section contains travel-related words and phrases you may find useful when going through customs and arranging for transportation.

English translation	*Pinyin*	Pronunciation	Chinese

Customs and Luggage

English translation	*Pinyin*	Pronunciation	Chinese
customs	*hǎiguān*	hai gwan	海关
duty	*guānshuì*	gwan shui	关税
health certificate	*jiànkāng zhèngmíngshū*	jien kang jreng ming shu	健康证明书
hotel	*fàndiàn/lǚguǎn*	fan dien/lui gwan	饭店、旅馆
interpreter	*fānyì*	fan yee	翻译
luggage	*xíngli*	shing lee	行李
passport control	*jiǎnyàn hùzhào*	jien yen hoo jrao	检验护照
passport	*hùzhào*	hoo jrao	护照
purse	*qiánbāo*	chien bao	钱包
room	*fángjiān*	fang jien	房间
tour bus	*lǚyóuchē*	lui you cheh	旅游车

English translation	Pinyin	Pronunciation	Chinese
tour group	*lǚxíngtuán*	lui shing twan	旅行团
tour guide	*dǎoyóu*	daw you	导游
travel agency	*lǚxíngshè*	lui shing sheh	旅行社
vacation	*dù jià*	doo jiah	度假
visa	*qiānzhèng*	chien jreng	签证
Here is my passport.	*zhè shì wǒ de hùzhào*	jre shr wo de hoo jrao	这是我的护照。
I am an American.	*wǒ shì Měiguó rén*	wo shr may gwo ren	我是美国人。
Australian	*Àodàlìyà rén*	aw dah lee yah ren	澳大利亚人
British	*Yīngguó rén*	ying gwo ren	英国人
Canadian	*Jiānádà rén*	jia nah dah ren	加拿大人
French	*Fǎguó rén*	fah gwo ren	法国人
German	*Déguó rén*	deh gwo ren	德国人
Italian	*Yìdàlì rén*	yee dah lee ren	意大利人
Japanese	*Rìběn rén*	rrr ben ren	日本人
Korean	*Hánguó rén*	han gwo ren	韩国人
I need an interpreter.	*wǒ xūyào yígè fānyì*	wo shuh yao yee geh fan yee	我需要一个翻译。

English translation	Pinyin	Pronunciation	Chinese
I am traveling alone.	*wǒ shì dāndú lǚxíng*	wo shr dan doo lui shing	我是单独旅行。
I am traveling with my wife.	*wǒ hé wǒ tàitai yìqǐ lǚxíng*	wo heh wo tai tai yee chee lui shing	我和我太太一起旅行。
my boy friend	*wǒ de nán péngyou*	wo de nan peng you	我的男朋友
my children	*wǒ de háizi*	wo de hai dzz	我的孩子
my daughter	*wǒ de nǚ'ér*	wo de nui er	我的女儿
my friend	*wǒ de péngyou*	wo de peng you	我的朋友
my girl friend	*wǒ de nǚ péngyou*	wo de nui peng you	我的女朋友
my husband	*wǒ de zhàngfu*	wo de jrang foo	我的丈夫
my son	*wǒ de érzi*	wo de er dzz	我的儿子
I am traveling with a group.	*wǒ shì suí tuán lǚxíng*	wo shr swei twan lui shing	我是随团旅行。
I am here on vacation.	*wǒ shì lái dùjià de*	wo shr lai doo jia de	我是来度假的。
I am here on business	*wǒ shì lái zuò shēngyì de*	wo shr lai dzwo sheng yee de	我是来做生意的。
I will stay for			
a few days.	*wǒ yào zhù jǐ tiān*	wo yao jroo gee tien	我要住几天。
a week	*yígè xīngqī*	yee guh shing chee	一个星期
a month	*yígè yuè*	yee guh yueh	一个月

English translation	Pinyin	Pronunciation	Chinese
a year	*yì nián*	yee nien	一年
Where is my luggage?	*wǒ de xíngli zài nǎr*	wo de shing lee dzai nar	我的行李在哪儿？
Here is my luggage.	*zhè shì wǒ de xíngli*	jre shr wo de shing lee	这是我的行李。
Shall I open my bag?	*yào wǒ dǎkāi bāo ma*	yao wo dah kai bao ma	要我打开包吗？
I have nothing to declare.	*wǒ méiyǒu shénme yào bàoguān de*	wo may you shen ma yao bao gwan de	我没有什么要报关的。
These are for my personal use.	*zhè dōu shì zì yòng de*	jre dou shr dzz yong de	这都是自用的。
These are small gifts.	*zhè shì xiē xiǎo lǐwù*	jre shr shieh shiao lee woo	这是些小礼物。
This is my camera.	*zhè shì wǒ de zhàoxiàngjī*	jre shr wo de jrao shiang gee	这是我的照相机。
Do I have to pay duty?	*wǒ yào fù shuì ma*	wo yao foo shui ma	我要付税吗？

English translation	*Pinyin*	Pronunciation	Chinese

Planes, Trains and Boats

English translation	*Pinyin*	Pronunciation	Chinese
airplane	*fēijī*	fay gee	飞机
airport	*fēijīchǎng*	fay gee chang	飞机场
behind schedule	*wǎn diǎn*	wan dien	晚点
beverage	*yǐnliào*	yin liao	饮料
blanket	*tǎnzi*	tan dzz	毯子
boarding pass	*dēng jī pái*	deng gee pai	登机牌
cabin	*chuán cāng*	chwan tsang	船舱
captain (boat)	*chuán zhǎng*	chwan jrang	船长
captain (plane)	*jī zhǎng*	gee jrang	机长
check-in	*jiǎn piào*	jien piao	检票
compartment	*chēxiāng*	che shiang	车箱
deck	*jiǎbǎn*	jia ban	甲板
departure time	*chūfā shíjiān*	chu fah shr jien	出发时间
dining car	*cānchē*	tsan cheh	餐车
dock	*mǎtóu*	mah tou	码头
economy class	*jīngjì cāng*	jing gee tsang	经济舱
electric fan	*diànshàn*	dien shan	电扇
enter the port	*jìn gǎng*	gin gang	进港

English translation	Pinyin	Pronunciation	Chinese
first-class	*tóu děng*	tou deng	头等
flight number	*hángbān hào*	hang ban hao	航班号
go ashore	*kào àn*	kao an	靠岸
hard seat (on train)	*yìng zuò*	ying dzwo	硬座
hard sleeper (on train)	*yìng wò*	ying wo	硬卧
landing (plane)	*zhuó lù*	jrwo lu	着陆
leave the port	*chū gǎng*	chu gang	出港
on schedule	*zhèng diǎn*	jreng dien	正点
on the ship	*zài chuán shàng*	dzai chwan shang	在船上
pillow	*zhěntou*	jren tow	枕头
plane ticket	*jīpiào*	gee piao	机票
platform ticket	*zhàntái piào*	jran tai piao	站台票
platform	*zhàntái*	jran tai	站台
sail	*hángxíng*	hang shing	航行
sailor	*chuányuán*	chwan yuen	船员
schedule	*shíkèbiǎo*	shr keh biao	时刻表
second-class	*èr děng*	er deng	二等
snack counter	*xiǎo mài bù*	shiao my boo	小卖部
soft sleeper (on train)	ruǎn wò	ruan wo	软卧

English translation	Pinyin	Pronunciation	Chinese
steamer	*lúnchuán*	lun chwan	轮船
take off	*qǐ fēi*	chee fay	起飞
ticket office	*shòupiàochù*	shou piao chu	售票处
train	*huǒchē*	hwo che	火车
train station	*huǒchēzhàn*	hwo che jran	火车站
waiting room (airport)	*hòujīshì*	hou gee shr	候机室
waiting room (boat)	*hòuchuánshì*	hou chwan shr	候船室
waiting room (train, bus)	*hòuchēshì*	hou che shr	候车室

Bus and Taxi

bus	*gōnggòng qìchē*	gong gong chee cheh	公共汽车
bus stop	*qìchēzhàn*	chee cheh jran	汽车站
driver	*sījī*	sse gee	司机
fare	*jiàqián*	jia chien	价钱
fast	*kuài*	kwai	快
last stop	*zhōngdiǎnzhàn*	jrung dien jran	终点站
left	*zuǒ*	dzwo	左

English translation	Pinyin	Pronunciation	Chinese
right	*yòu*	you	右
slow	*màn*	man	慢
straight ahead	*yìzhí zǒu*	yee jrr dzou	一直走
subway station	*dìtiězhàn*	dee tieh jran	地铁站
taxi	*chūzūchē*	chu dzoo cheh	出租车
Could you call me a taxi?	*qǐng bāng wǒ jiào yí liàng chūzūchē*	ching bang wo jiao yee liang chu dzoo cheh	请帮我叫一辆出租车。
Where can I get a taxi?	*nǎlǐ yǒu chūzū qìchē*	nah lee you chu dzoo chee cheh	哪里有出租汽车？
How far away is the hotel?	*lǚguǎn yǒu duō yuǎn*	lui gwan you dwo yuen	旅馆有多远？
How long would it take to get there?	*duō cháng shíjiān néng dào*	dwo chang shr jien neng dao	多长时间能到？
Can you wait for me?	*nǐ néng děng wǒ ma*	nee neng deng wo ma	你能等我吗？
Please take me to the hotel.	*qǐng sòng wǒ huí lǚguǎn*	ching song wo hwei lui gwan	请送我回旅馆。
Please take me to this address.	*qǐng dài wǒ dào zhège dìfāng*	ching dai wo dao jre geh dee fang	请带我到这个地方。
Where is the bus stop?	*qìchēzhàn zài nǎr*	chee cheh jran dzai nar	汽车站在哪儿？

Getting Around Town

Tourists who travel around China by themselves always find it quite an adventure to do so, especially when they speak very little, or no Chinese at all. In some major Chinese cities, foreigners can expect to bump into someone who speaks English. In fact, there are thousands of Chinese students who study English at schools. Many of them are eager to find a foreigner to practice English with. However, help may not always be on the way when you need it. For those of you who do plan to travel alone, this section offers some useful and handy words and phrases on direction, signs, city names, and so on. You can ask any Chinese for help by simply pointing at the words or sentences you wish to say.

At the end of the section is a list of tourist attractions in Beijing, Shanghai, Hangzhou, Nanjing, Guilin and Guangzhou.

English translation	*Pinyin*	Pronunciation	Chinese

Around Town

alley	*hútòngr*	hoo tong er	胡同儿
boat	*chuán*	chwan	船
bridge	*qiáo*	chiao	桥
cave	*dòng*	dong	洞
city	*chéngshì*	cheng shr	城市
countryside	*nóngcūn*	nong tsun	农村
direction	*fāngxiàng*	fang shiang	方向
downstairs	*lóu xià*	low shiah	楼下
east	*dōng*	doong	东
garden	*huāyuán*	hwa yuan	花园
grocery store	*shípǐndiàn*	shr pin dien	食品店
guide	*dǎoyóu*	dao you	导游
hill	*xiǎo shān*	shiao shan	小山
island	*dǎo*	dao	岛
lake	*hú*	hoo	湖
left	*zuǒ*	dzwo	左
main street	*zhǔyào jiēdào*	jru yao jieh dao	主要街道
map	*dìtú*	dee too	地图

English translation	*Pinyin*	Pronunciation	Chinese
monastery	*sì*	sse	寺
north	*běi*	bay	北
pagoda	*tǎ*	tah	塔
park	*gōngyuán*	gong yuan	公园
pavilion	*tíng*	ting	亭
pedestrian crossing	*rén xíng héng dào*	ren shing hung dao	人行横道
post office	*yóujú*	you juh	邮局
right	*yòu*	you	右
river	*hé*	huh	河
road	*lù*	loo	路
scenic spot	*fēngjǐngdiǎn*	feng jing dien	风景点
sidewalk	*biàndào*	bien dao	便道
south	*nán*	nan	南
square	*guǎngchǎng*	gwang chang	广场
straight ahead	*yìzhí zǒu*	yee jrr dzoh	一直走
street	*jiēdào*	jieh dao	街道
temple	*miào*	miao	庙
traffic lights	*hónglǜdēng*	hong lui deng	红绿灯
upstairs	*lóu shàng*	low shang	楼上
west	*xī*	shee	西
zoo	*dòngwùyuán*	dong woo yuan	动物园

English translation	Pinyin	Pronunciation	Chinese
Can you help me?	*nǐ néng bāngzhù wǒ ma*	nee neng bang jru wo ma	你能帮助我吗？
I am lost.	*wǒ mí lù le*	wo mee loo le	我迷路了。
What is our itinerary?	*wǒmen de xíngchéng shì shénme*	wo men de shing cheng shr shen ma	我们的行程是什么？
Do you have a city map?	*nǐ yǒu shìqū dìtú ma*	nee you shr chu dee too ma	你有市区地图吗？
Where is the restroom?	*cèsuǒ zài nǎli*	tse swo dzai nah lee	厕所在哪里？
Where is the post office?	*yóujú zài nǎli*	you ju dzai nah lee	邮局在哪里？
Where is our group?	*wǒmen de tuán duì zài nǎli*	wo men de twan dway dzai nah lee	我们的团队在哪里？
Could you show me the way to Beijing Hotel?	*nǐ néng gàosu wǒ qù Běijīng fàndiàn zěnme zǒu ma*	nee neng gao su wo chu bay jing fan dien dzen ma dzoh ma	你能告诉我去北京饭店怎么走吗？
I am tired.	*wǒ lèi le*	wo lay le	我累了。
Let us have a rest.	*wǒmen xiūxi yíxià ba*	wo men shio shee yee shiah ba	我们休息一下吧。
What are the local attractions?	*zhèlǐ yǒu shénme míngshèng*	jreh lee you shen ma ming sheng	这里有什么名胜？

English translation	Pinyin	Pronunciation	Chinese
We would like to visit a school.	*wǒmen xiǎng cānguān yìsuǒ xuéxiào*	wo men shiang tsan gwan yee suo shueh shiao	我们想参观一所学校。
museum	*bówùguǎn*	bo woo gwan	博物馆
church	*jiàotáng*	jiao tang	教堂
library	*túshūguǎn*	too shu gwan	图书馆
shopping center	*gòuwù zhōngxīn*	go woo jrung shin	购物中心
Can I take a picture?	*wǒ kěyǐ zhàoxiàng ma*	wo keh yee jraw shiang ma	我可以照相吗？

Reading the Signs

caution	*xiǎoxīn*	shiao shin	小心
closed	*guānmén*	gwan men	关门
danger	*wēixiǎn*	way shien	危险
Do not enter	*jìnzhǐ rù nèi*	gin jrr roo nay	禁止入内
Don't touch	*qǐng wù chùmō*	ching woo choo maw	请勿触摸
elevator	*diàntī*	dien tee	电梯
emergency exit	*jǐnjí chūkǒu*	gin gee choo koh	紧急出口
entrance	*jìnkǒu, rùkǒu*	gin koh, roo koh	进口，入口
exit	*chūkǒu*	choo koh	出口

English translation	Pinyin	Pronunciation	Chinese
for rent	*chūzū*	choo dzoo	出租
for sale	*dài shòu*	dai show	待售
keep out	*qiè wù rù nèi*	chieh woo roo nay	切勿入内
ladies room	*nǚ cèsuǒ*	nuh tse swo	女厕所
lounge	*xiūxishì*	shio shee shr	休息室
men's room	*nán cèsuǒ*	nan tse swo	男厕所
no admittance	*jìnzhǐ rù nèi*	gin jrr roo nay	禁止入内
no smoking	*jìnzhǐ xīyān*	gin jrr shee yan	禁止吸烟
no photos	*jìnzhǐ zhàoxiàng*	gin jrr jraw shiang	禁止照相
no swimming	*jìnzhǐ yóuyǒng*	gin jrr you yong	禁止游泳
sale	*chūshòu*	choo show	出售
service desk	*fúwùtái*	foo woo tai	服务台
sold out	*mài wán le*	my wan le	卖完了
telephone	*diànhuà*	dien hwah	电话

Factories and Schools

art school	*yìshù xuéyuàn*	yee shu shue yuan	艺术学院
bonus	*jiǎngjīn*	jiang gin	奖金
day care center	*tuó'ér suǒ*	tuo er swo	托儿所
factory	*gōngchǎng*	gong chang	工厂

English translation	*Pinyin*	Pronunciation	Chinese
factory director	*chǎngzhǎng*	chang jrang	厂长
foreign investment	*wàiguó tóuzī*	why gwo toh dzz	外国投资
income	*shōurù*	show roo	收入
institute	*xuéyuàn*	shue yuan	学院
joint venture	*hézī qǐyè*	huh dzz chee yeh	合资企业
kindergarten	*yòu ér yuán*	you er yuan	幼儿园
medical school	*yīxuéyuàn*	yee shue yuan	医学院
middle school	*zhōngxué*	jrong shue	中学
music school	*yīnyuè xuéyuàn*	yin yueh shue yuan	音乐学院
parents	*jiāzhǎng, fùmǔ*	jia jrang, foo moo	家长，父母
pension	*tuìxiūjīn*	twei show gin	退休金
play ground	*yùndòngchǎng*	yun dong chang	运动场
primary school	*xiǎoxué*	shiao shue	小学
privatization	*sīyǒuhuà*	sse you hwa	私有化
products	*chǎnpǐn*	chan pin	产品
professor	*jiàoshòu*	jiao show	教授
state-run factory	*guóyíng gōngchǎng*	gwo ying gong chang	国营工厂
student	*xuéshēng*	shue sheng	学生
teacher	*lǎoshī*	lao shr	老师
teacher's college	*shīfàn xuéyuàn*	shr fan shue yuan	师范学院
trade union	*gōnghuì*	gong hwei	工会

English translation	*Pinyin*	Pronunciation	Chinese
university	*dàxué*	dah shue	大学
wage	*gōngzī*	gong dzz	工资
worker	*gōngrén*	gong ren	工人
workshop	*chējiān*	cheh jien	车间

Animals and Flowers

apple tree	*píngguǒ shù*	ping gwo shoo	苹果树
bird	*niǎo*	niao	鸟
cat	*māo*	mao	猫
chicken	*jī*	gee	鸡
cow	*niú*	nioh	牛
chrysanthemum	*júhuā*	ju hwa	菊花
deer	*lù*	loo	鹿
dog	*gǒu*	goh	狗
donkey	*lǘ*	lui	驴
duck	*yā*	yah	鸭
gold fish	*jīnyú*	gin yu	金鱼
horse	*mǎ*	mah	马
insect	*chóng*	chung	虫

English translation	*Pinyin*	Pronunciation	Chinese
orange tree	*júzi shù*	ju dzz shoo	橘子树
panda	*xióngmāo*	shiung mao	熊猫
peach tree	*táo shù*	tao shoo	桃树
pig	*zhū*	jroo	猪
rabbit	*tù*	too	兔
rice field	*dàotián*	dao tien	稻田
rose	*méiguì*	may gwei	玫瑰
water buffalo	*shuǐniú*	shui nioh	水牛
watermelon	*xīguā*	shee gwah	西瓜
wheat field	*màitián*	my tien	麦田

City Names

Beihai	*běihǎi*	bay hai	北海
Beijing	*Běijīng*	bay jing	北京
Dalian	*dàlián*	dah lien	大连
Fuzhou	*fúzhōu*	foo jroh	福州
Guilin	*guìlín*	gwei lin	桂林
Hainan Island	*hǎinándǎo*	hai nan dao	海南岛
Hangzhou	*hángzhōu*	hang jroh	杭州
Lianyungang	*liányúngǎng*	lien yun gang	连云港

English translation	Pinyin	Pronunciation	Chinese
Nanjing	*nánjīng*	nan jing	南京
Nantong	*nántōng*	nan tong	南通
Ningbo	*níngbō*	ning baw	宁波
Qingdao	*qīngdǎo*	ching dao	青岛
Qinhuangdao	*qínhuángdǎo*	chin hwang dao	秦皇岛
Shanghai	*shànghǎi*	shang hai	上海
Suzhou	*sūzhōu*	soo jroh	苏州
Tianjin	*tiānjīn*	tien gin	天津
Wenzhou	*wēnzhōu*	wen jroh	温州
Wuhan	*wǔhàn*	woo han	武汉
Wuxi	*wúxī*	woo shee	无锡
Xian	*xī'ān*	shee an	西安
Yantai	*yāntái*	yan tie	烟台
Zhanjiang	*zhànjiāng*	jran jiang	湛江

Tourist Attractions in Various Cities

1. Beijing

Beihai Park	*Běihǎi gōngyuán*	bay hai gong yuan	北海公园
Beijing Zoo	*Běijīng dòngwu-yuán*	bay jing dong woo yuan	北京动物园

English translation	Pinyin	Pronunciation	Chinese
Forbidden City	*Zǐjìnchéng (gùgōng)*	dzz gin cheng (goo gong)	紫禁城（故宫）
Fragrance Hill	*Xiāngshān*	shiang shan	香山
Great Hall of the People	*Rénmín dàhuìtáng*	ren min dah hwei tang	人民大会堂
Marco Polo Bridge	*Lúgōuqiáo*	loo goh chiao	卢沟桥
Summer Palace	*Yíhéyuán*	yee huh yuan	颐和园
Temple of Heaven	*Tiāntán*	tien tan	天坛
The Great Wall	*Chángchéng*	chang cheng	长城
The Ming Tombs	*Shísānlíng*	shr san ling	十三陵
Tiananmen Square	*Tiānānmén guǎngchǎng*	tien an men gwang chang	天安门广场
Wangfujing Street	*Wángfǔjǐng dàjiē*	wang foo jing dah jieh	王府井大街

2. Shanghai

English translation	Pinyin	Pronunciation	Chinese
Huaihai Road	*Huáihǎi lù*	hwai hai loo	淮海路
Lu Xun Museum	*Lǔxùn jìniànguǎn*	loo shun gee nien gwan	鲁迅纪念馆
Nanjing Road	*Nánjīng lù*	nan jing loo	南京路

English translation	Pinyin	Pronunciation	Chinese
People's Square	*Rénmín guǎngchǎng*	ren min gwang chang	人民广场
Pudong New District	*Púdōng xīn qū*	poo dong shin chu	蒲东新区
Temple of the Jade Buddha	*Yùfósì*	yu fow sse	玉佛寺
The Bund	*wàitān*	wai tan	外滩
Yu Garden	*Yùyuán*	yu yuan	豫园

3. Hangzhou

English translation	Pinyin	Pronunciation	Chinese
Bai Causeway	*Báidí*	bai dee	白堤
Dragon's Well	*Lóngjǐng*	long jing	龙井
Lingyin Temple	*Língyǐnsì*	lin yin sse	灵隐寺
Pagoda of the Six Harmonies	*Liùhétǎ*	liu huh tah	六和塔
Su Causeway	*Sūdí*	soo dee	苏堤
Three Pools That Mirror the Moon	*sān tán yìng yuè*	san tan ying yueh	三潭映月
Tiger Run Spring	*Hǔpǎoquán*	hoo pao chuan	虎跑泉
Viewing Fish at Flower Harbor	*huāgǎng guān yú*	hwa gang gwan yu	花港观鱼

English translation	Pinyin	Pronunciation	Chinese
West Lake	*Xīhú*	shee hoo	西湖

4. Nanjing

English translation	Pinyin	Pronunciation	Chinese
Drum Tower	*Gǔlóu*	goo loh	鼓楼
Lake Xuan Wu	*Xuánwǔhú*	shuan woo hoo	玄武湖
Ling Gu Temple	*Línggǔsì*	ling goo sse	灵谷寺
Nanjing Museum	*Nánjīng bówùguǎn*	nan jing bo woo gwan	南京博物馆
Sun Yat-sen's Mausoleum	*Zhōngshānlíng*	jrung shan ling	中山陵
Tomb of Emperor Ming Xiao	*Míngxiào líng*	ming shiao ling	明孝陵
Yangtze River Bridge	*Chángjiāng dàqiáo*	chang jiang dah chiao	长江大桥
Yangtze River	*Chángjiāng*	chang jiang	长江
Yu Hua Tai	*Yǔhuātái*	yu hwa tai	雨花台

5. Guilin

English translation	Pinyin	Pronunciation	Chinese
Crescent Hill	*Yuèyá shān*	yueh yah shan	月牙山

English translation	Pinyin	Pronunciation	Chinese
Elephant Trunk Hill	Xiàng bí shān	shiang bee shan	象鼻山
Lijiang River	*Líjiāng*	lee jiang	漓江
Pagoda Hill	*Tǎ shān*	tah shan	塔山
Reed Pipe Cave	*Lúdí yán*	loo dee yan	芦笛岩
Seven Star Hill	*Qī xīng yán*	chee shing yan	七星岩
Solitary Beauty Peak	*Dúxiù fēng*	doo shiu feng	独秀峰
Yang Shuo	*Yángshuò*	yang shwo	阳朔

6. Guangzhou

Foreign Trade Center	*Wàimào zhōngxīn*	wai mao jrong shin	外贸中心
Guangzhou Cultural Park	*Guǎngzhōu wénhuà gōngyuán*	gwang jroh wen hwa gong yuan	广州文化公园
Liuhua Park	*Liú huā gōngyuán*	lew hwa gong yuan	流花公园
White Cloud Mountains	*Báiyún shān*	bye yun shan	白云山
Zhenhai Pavilion	*Zhèn hǎi lóu*	jren hai loh	镇海楼

English translation	*Pinyin*	Pronunciation	Chinese
Zhongshan Memorial Hall	*Zhōngshān táng*	jrong shan tang	中山堂

7. In the Vicinity of Guangzhou

English translation	*Pinyin*	Pronunciation	Chinese
Conghua Hot Springs	*Cónghuà wēnquán*	tsong hwa wen	从化温泉
Foshan City	*Fóshān shì*	fo shan shr	佛山市
Shantou	*Shàntóu*	shan toh	汕头
Shenzhen	*Shēnzhèn*	shen jren	深圳
Zhaoqing City	*Zhàoqìng shì*	jrao ching shr	肇庆市
Zhuhai	*Zhūhǎi*	jroo hai	珠海

Communication

A few years ago, making a phone call in China could be rather frustrating. Due to the limited phone service available, one could spend hours looking for a public phone on the street. At that time, telephones were installed only in state-run work places and at the homes of high-ranking officials. Residential phones for ordinary people were unheard of. Even if one had access to a phone, he would have a lot of difficulty getting through, for the lines were too old to function properly.

Fortunately, there have been great improvements in China's telecommunication system in recent years. Old phone lines have been replaced with new ones nationwide. The number of phones is now many times that of several years ago. Residential phone service can be applied for by everyone, provided that he pays a staggering installation fee of 5,000 yuan or more and bears with a six-month, or longer, waiting period.

Fax machines are very much limited to government offices. Individuals are not allowed to own a fax machine at home, although the restrictions are not strictly enforced. In many organizations where fax machines are installed, the machines are open only during work hours. They are turned off at night. For Americans who wish to send a fax to China, they need to constantly remind their Chinese partners to leave the fax machine on after work so that the fax can be sent at a convenient time.

In comparision, postal service is more efficient in China. For those who wish to send letters or parcels back to America, this section provides the necessary words and phrases in such situations.

English translation	Pinyin	Pronunciation	Chinese

At the Post Office

English translation	Pinyin	Pronunciation	Chinese
addressee	*shōu xìn rén*	shou shin ren	收信人
airmail	*hángkōng*	hang kung	航空
envelope	*xìnfēng*	shin feng	信封
express mail	*kuàijiàn*	kwai jien	快件
glue	*jiànghu*	jiang hoo	浆糊
mail box	*xìnxiāng*	shin shiang	信箱
overweight	*chāo zhòng*	chao jrung	超重
parcel	*bāoguǒ*	bao gwo	包裹
post office	*yóujú*	you ju	邮局

English translation	Pinyin	Pronunciation	Chinese
postage due	*qiàn yóuzī*	chien you dzz	欠邮资
postcard	*míngxìnpiàn*	ming shin pien	明信片
postman	*yóudìyuán*	you dee yuan	邮递员
postmark	*yóuchuō*	you chwo	邮戳
registered mail	*guàhàoxìn*	gwa hao shin	挂号信
remittance	*huìkuǎn*	hwei kwan	汇款
sealed	*fēngkǒu*	feng koh	封口
sender	*jì xìn rén*	gee shin ren	寄信人
stamps	*yóupiào*	you piao	邮票
stationery	*xìnzhǐ*	shin jrr	信纸
surface mail	*píng yóu*	ping you	平邮
telegram	*diànbào*	dien bao	电报
telex	*diànchuán*	dien chwan	电传
to send a letter	*jì xìn*	gee shin	寄信
urgent telegram	*jiājí diànbào*	jiah gee dien bao	加急电报
zip code	*yóu biān*	you bien	邮编
I want to send a letter.	*wǒ xiǎng jì yì fēng xìn*	wo shiang gee yee feng shin	我想寄一封信。
I want to sent a letter to America.	*wǒ xiǎng jì yì fēng xìn dào Měiguó*	wo shiang gee yee feng shin dao may gwo	我想寄一封信到美国。

English translation	Pinyin	Pronunciation	Chinese
I would like to send a telegram.	*wǒ xiǎng fā yìfèn diànbào*	wo shiang fah yee fen dien bao	我想发一份电报。
Here is the address.	*zhè shì dìzhǐ*	jre shr dee jrr	这是地址。
How much is it to send to America?	*jìdào Měiguó yào duōshǎo qián*	gee dao may gwo yao dwo shao chien	寄到美国要多少钱？

Telephone

collect call	*shòufù diànhuà*	shou foo dien hwa	授付电话
international call	*guójì chángtú*	gwo gee chang too	国际长途
local call	*dāngdì diànhuà*	dang dee dien hwa	当地电话
long distance call	*chángtú diànhuà*	chang too dien hwa	长途电话
operator	*zǒngjī*	dzung gee	总机
public phone	*gōngyòng diànhuà*	gong yong dien hwa	公用电话
telephone	*diànhuà*	dien hwa	电话
telephone number	*diànhuà hàomǎ*	dien hwa hao mah	电话号码
to make a phone call	*dǎ diànhuà*	dah dien hwa	打电话
I want to call Mr. Li.	*wǒ xiǎng gěi Lǐ xiān- sheng dǎ ge diànhuà*	wo shiang gay lee shien sheng dah guh dien hwa	我想给李先生打个电话。
May I use your phone?	*wǒ kěyǐ jiè yòng nǐ de diànhuà ma*	wo kuh yee jieh yong nee de dien hwa ma	我可以借用你的电话吗？

English	Pinyin	Pronunciation	Chinese
I want to make a call to America.	wǒ xiǎng dǎ ge diànhuà dào Měiguó	wo shiang dah guh dien hwa dao may gwo	我想打个电话到美国。
How much is it per minute?	yì fēn zhōng duōshǎo qián	yee fen jrung dwo shao chien	一分钟多少钱？
May I speak to Mr. Wang?	wǒ zhǎo Wáng xiānsheng	wo jrao wang shien sheng	我找王先生。
He is not here.	tā bú zài	tah boo dzai	他不在。
I can't hear you.	wǒ tīng bù qīng	wo ting boo ching	我听不清。
Please speak louder.	qǐng dà shēng diǎn	ching dah sheng dien	请大声点。
Please speak slowly.	qǐng shuō màn yìdiǎn	ching shwo man yee dien	请说慢一点。
Do you speak English?	nǐ shuō Yīngyǔ ma	nee shwo ying yu ma	你说英语吗？
My number is...	wǒ de hàomǎ shì...	wo de hao ma shr...	我的号码是。
Please dial again.	qǐng zài bō yíbiàn	ching dzai bo yee bien	请再拨一遍。
You have the wrong number.	nǐ de hàomǎ cuò le	nee de hao ma tswo le	你的号码错了。
The line is busy.	zhàn xiàn	jran shien	占线。
There is no answer.	méi rén jiē	may ren jieh	没人接。

At The Bank

The Chinese currency is called *renminbi* (RMB), which literally means "people's money." The basic unit of RMB is *yuan*, equivalent to a dollar in unit, not in value. Like in America, where a dollar is called a "buck," the Chinese have different names for their currency as well. A *yuan* is often referred to as *"kuai,"* which literally means a "piece." The smallest unit in RMB is the *fen*, equivalent to a cent. Ten *fen* is called one *jiao*, or *mao*. Chinese banknotes come in 100, 50 , 10, 5, 2 and 1 *yuan* notes, and coins come in 5, 2 and 1 fen denominations.

Upon arrival in China, you can change your money into RMB at airports, hotels, friendship stores, or at a Bank of China branch. Before 1995, foreigners were required to carry foreign exchange certificate (FEC), which in theory had the same value as RMB, but in fact had much higher value on the black market, causing a lot of social problems. By the end of 1994, the Chinese government finally decided to get rid of FEC, putting an end to the co-existence of a dual currency system.

English translation	*Pinyin*	Pronunciation	Chinese
bank	*yínháng*	yin hang	银行
bankdraft	*yínháng huìpiào*	yin hang hwei piao	银行汇票
banknote	*chāopiào*	chao piao	钞票
cash a check	*zhīpiào duìxiàn*	jrr piao dwei shien	支票兑现
cash	*xiànjīn*	shien gin	现金
cashier	*shōu yín yuán*	shou yin yuan	收银员
change money	*duìhuàn*	dwei hwan	兑换
credit card	*xìnyòngkǎ*	shin yong kah	信用卡
exchange	*duìhuàn*	dwei hwan	兑换
exchange rate	*duìhuànlǜ*	dwei hwan lui	兑换率
fen	*fēn*	fen	分
interest	*lìxi*	lee shee	利息
interest rate	*lìlǜ*	lee lui	利率
jiao	*jiǎo*	jiao	角
kuai	*kuài*	kwai	块
mao	*máo*	mao	毛
money	*qián*	chien	钱
renminbi	*rénmínbì*	ren min bee	人民币
signature	*qiānzì*	chien dzz	签字
small change	*língqián*	lin chien	零钱
travelers' cheque	*lǚxíng zhīpiào*	lui shing jrr piao	旅行支票

English translation	Pinyin	Pronunciation	Chinese
yuan	*yuán*	yuan	元
I want to change some money.	*wǒ xiǎng duìhuàn diǎn qián*	wo shiang dwei hwan dian chien	我想兑换点钱。
I want to change travellers' checks.	*wǒ xiǎng duìhuàn lǚxíng zhīpiào*	wo shiang dwei hwan lui shing jrr piao	我想兑换旅行支票
I want to change some US dollars.	*wǒ xiǎng duìhuàn diǎn měiyuán*	wo shiang dwei hwan dien may yuan	我想兑换点美元。
French francs	*fǎláng*	fah lang	法郎
Japanese yen	*rìyuán*	rr yuan	日元
UK pounds	*yīngbàng*	ying bang	英镑
HK dollar	*gǎngbì*	gang bee	港币
Canadian dollar	*jiābì*	jia bee	加币
Deutschmarks	*mǎkè*	mah kuh	马克
What is the exchange rate?	*huìlǜ shì duōshǎo*	hwei lui shrr dwo shao	汇率是多少?
What time does it open?	*jǐ diǎn kāi mén*	gee dien kai men	几点开门?
What time does it close?	*jǐ diǎn guān mén*	gee dien gwan men	几点关门?
Do you accept credit cards?	*kěyǐ yòng xìn-yòngkǎ ma*	kuh yee yong shin yong kah ma	可以用信用卡吗?

English translation	Pinyin	Pronunciation	Chinese
This is my signature.	*zhè shì wǒ de qiānzì*	jre shrr wo de chien dzz	这是我的签字。
This is not my signature.	*zhè bú shì wǒ de qiānzì*	jre boo shrr wo de chien dzz	这不是我的签字。
Please give me a 50 yuan note.	*qǐng gěi wǒ wǔshí yuán de chāopiào*	ching gay wo woo shrr yuan de chao piao	请给我五十元的钞票。
I would like to open an account.	*wǒ xiǎng kāi yígè zhànghù*	wo shiang kai yee guh jrang hoo	我想开一个帐户。
I would like to deposit some money.	*wǒ xiǎng cún qián*	wo shiang tsun chien	我想存钱。
I would like to withdraw some money.	*wǒ xiǎng qǔ qián*	wo shiang chui chien	我想取钱。

At The Hotel

The last ten years have seen a soaring number of luxury hotels catering to foreign tourists in most major Chinese cities. Those of you who are on a tour will most likely stay in such hotels, where the need to speak Chinese is rather minimal. However, if you are traveling alone on a tight budget, you may want to stay in some of the less expensive hotels, where you would definitely need to speak Chinese in order to communicate.

Like in America, hotels in China are divided into different categories. Luxury hotels are called *fàndiàn* (饭店) or *bīnguǎn* (宾馆), and normally cater to foreign tourists or businesspeople. The midrange hotels with minimum service are called *lǚguǎn* (旅馆), most of which are not accessible for foreigners. At the very bottom is *lǚshè* (旅社) or *zhāodàisuǒ* (招待所), which are normally for Chinese only. Another form of accommodation is public bathrooms, which take in customers at night for a very low price. Foreigners won't even have a chance to find where they are.

Prices for different hotels vary enormously. Don't be surprised if the luxury hotels charge you more than you pay an equivalent hotel in the United States. However, if you join a tour group and pay a package price, you need not worry about the price. Like everywhere else, travel agencies in China can obtain a fairly cheap price from hotels.

English translation	Pinyin	Pronunciation	Chinese
address	*dìzhǐ*	dee jrr	地址
air conditioner	*kōngtiáo*	kung tiao	空调
ashtray	*yānhuīgāng*	yan hwei gong	烟灰缸
bath	*xǐzǎo*	shee dzao	洗澡
bed	*chuáng*	chwang	床
bill	*zhàngdān*	jrang dan	帐单
blanket	*tǎnzi*	tan dzz	毯子
cafe	*kāfēi tīng*	kah fay ting	咖啡厅
candle	*làzhú*	la jroo	蜡烛
carpet	*dìtǎn*	dee tan	地毯
chair	*yǐzi*	yee dzz	椅子
clean	*gānjìng*	gan jing	干净
dining room	*cāntīng*	tsan ting	餐厅
dirty	*zāng*	dzang	脏
double room	*shuāngrénjiān*	shuang ren jien	双人间
drinking water	*yǐnyòngshuǐ*	yin yong shui	饮用水

English translation	Pinyin	Pronunciation	Chinese
dry cleaning	*gānxǐ*	gan shee	干洗
electric fan	*diànshàn*	dien shan	电扇
electricity	*diàn*	dien	电
elevator	*diàntī*	dien tee	电梯
front desk	*qiántái*	chien tai	前台
guest house	*bīnguǎn*	bin gwan	宾馆
hanger	*yījià*	yee jia	衣架
heating	*nuǎnqì*	nwan chee	暖气
hot water	*rèshuǐ*	re shui	热水
hotel	*fàndiàn/lǚguǎn*	fan dien/lui gwan	饭店、旅馆
key	*yàoshi*	yao shr	钥匙
laundry	*xǐyīfu*	shee yee foo	洗衣服
lobby	*qiántīng*	chien ting	前厅
lock	*suǒ*	swo	锁
mattress	*chuángdiàn*	chwang dien	床垫
mirror	*jìngzi*	jing dzz	镜子
pillow	*zhěntou*	jren tow	枕头
price	*jiàqián*	jia chien	价钱
quiet	*ānjìng*	an jing	安静
quilt	*bèizi*	bay dzz	被子
registration	*dēngjì*	deng gee	登记

English translation	Pinyin	Pronunciation	Chinese
reservation	*yùdìng*	yu ding	预订
room number	*fángjiānhào*	fang jien hao	房间号
service desk	*fúwùtái*	foo woo tai	服务台
sheet	*chuángdān*	chwang dan	床单
shop	*xiǎomàibù*	shiao my boo	小卖部
shower	*línyù*	lin yu	淋浴
single room	*dānrénjiān*	dan ren jien	单人间
soap	*féizào*	fay dzao	肥皂
stairs	*lóutī*	low tee	楼梯
suitcase	*yīxiāng*	yee shiang	衣箱
suite	*tàojiān*	tao jien	套间
table	*zhuōzi*	jrwo dzz	桌子
television	*diànshì*	dien shr	电视
toilet paper	*wèishēngzhǐ*	way sheng jrr	卫生纸
towel	*máojīn*	mao gin	毛巾
window	*chuāngzi*	chwang dzz	窗子

| What's the name of this hotel? | *zhège fàndiàn jiào shénme míngzi* | jre guh fan dien jiao shen ma ming dzz | 这个饭店叫什么名字? |
| I would like a single room | *wǒ xiǎng yào yígè dānrén fáng* | wo shiang yao yee guh dan ren fang | 我想要一个单人房。 |

English translation	Pinyin	Pronunciation	Chinese
What is the price?	*duōshǎo qián*	dwo shao chien	多少钱？
My reservation number is...	*wǒ de dìng fáng hào shì...*	wo de ding fang hao shrr...	我的订房号是
I will stay for one night.	*wǒ zhù yígè wǎnshàng*	wo jroo yee guh wan shang	我住一个晚上。
two nights	*liǎng gè wǎnshàng*	liang guh wan shang	两个晚上
a week	*yígè xīngqī*	yee guh shing chee	一个星期
May I see the room?	*wǒ kěyǐ kànkan fángjiān ma*	wo keh yee kan kan fang jien ma	我可以看看房间吗？
I don't like this room.	*wǒ bùxǐhuān zhèige fángjiān*	wo boo shee hwan jre guh fang jien	我不喜欢这个房间。
It's too expensive.	*tài guì le*	tai gwei le	太贵了。
too big	*tài dà le*	tai da le	太大了
too cold	*tài lěng le*	tai leng le	太冷了
too dark	*tài àn le*	tai an le	太暗了
too noisy	*tài chǎo le*	tai chao le	太吵了
too small	*tài xiǎo le*	tai shiao le	太小了
Do you have a cheaper room?	*yǒu gèng piányi de fángjiān ma*	you gen pien yee de fang jien ma	有更便宜的房间吗？
The toilet doesn't work.	*cèsuǒ huài le*	tse swo hwai le	厕所坏了。

English translation	Pinyin	Pronunciation	Chinese
Can I change rooms?	*kěyǐ huàn yígè fángjiān ma*	keh yee hwan yee guh fang jien ma	可以换一个房间吗？
Is there a message for me?	*yǒu wǒ de liúyán ma*	you wo de lew yan ma	有我的留言吗？
I am leaving tomorrow.	*wǒ míngtiān zǒu*	wo ming tien dzou	我明天走。
Pleake wake me up at 6:00 a.m.	*qǐng míngtiān zǎo shàng liù diǎn jiào xǐng wǒ*	ching ming tien dzao shang lew dien jiao shing wo	请明天早上六点叫醒我。

Eating Out

For thousands of years, food has been one of the primary concerns of the Chinese people. The reason is simple: there has never been enough. Throughout Chinese history, hunger has been one of the major causes of human death. Therefore, it is a tremendous achievement for the Chinese to have basically solved the problem of food and clothes for its 1.2 billion people today.

Paradoxically, the waste of food in China cannot be matched by any other country in the world. When the Chinese throw banquets to entertain guests, the food served could be several times more than enough. The left-overs are often thrown away. People do this because they try to show their generosity by serving more food than is enough to stuff their guests.

Because of the importance the Chinese have attached to eating, a variety of cooking styles have been developed. Statistics show that the number of well-known dishes alone is well over 8,000. The making of the finest food has been elevated into an art form. Sometimes at state banquets, people would hardly want to touch the food for fear of ruining a beautiful piece of art work.

For foreign tourists, eating Chinese food could be one of the most memorable experiences of their China tour. The following words and phrases will help you choose from the many dishes on a restaurant menu.

English translation	*Pinyin*	Pronunciation	Chinese

At the Restaurant

English translation	*Pinyin*	Pronunciation	Chinese
beer	*píjiǔ*	pee geo	啤酒
bowl	*wǎn*	wan	碗
brandy	*báilándì*	bye lan dee	白兰地
breakfast	*zǎocān*	dzao tsan	早餐
broil	*kǎo*	kao	烤
Cantonese restaurant	*Guǎngdōngguǎnr*	gwang dong gwan	广东馆儿
cheers	*gānbēi*	gan bay	干杯
Chinese food	*zhōng cān*	jrong tsan	中餐
chopsticks	*kuàizi*	kwai dzz	筷子
coffee	*kāfēi*	kah fay	咖啡
cup	*bēizi*	bay dzz	杯子
deep fry	*zhá*	jrah	炸

English translation	Pinyin	Pronunciation	Chinese
delicious	hěn hǎo chī	hen hao chrr	很好吃
dining room	cāntīng	tsan ting	餐厅
dinner	wǎncān	wan tsan	晚餐
dish	cài	tsai	菜
fork	chāzi	chah dzz	叉子
fresh	xīnxiān	shin shien	新鲜
frozen	lěng dòng de	leng dong de	冷冻的
fry	jiān	jien	煎
garlic	suàn	swen	蒜
ginger	jiāng	jiang	姜
glass	bōli bēi	baw lee bay	玻璃杯
green tea	lǜ chá	lui chah	绿茶
hot (spicy)	là	lah	辣
ice water	bīng shuǐ	bing shui	冰水
iced beer	bīng zhèn píjiǔ	bing jren pee geo	冰镇啤酒
jasmine tea	mòlìhuā chá	maw lee hua chah	茉莉花茶
juice	guǒ zhī	gwo jrr	果汁
knife	dāozi	dao dzz	刀子
lunch	wǔcān	woo tsan	午餐
Mandarin restaurant	běifāngguǎn	bay fang gwan	北方馆

English translation	Pinyin	Pronunciation	Chinese
menu	càidān	tsai dan	菜单
mineral water	kuàngquán shuǐ	kwang chuan shui	矿泉水
napkin	cānjīn zhǐ	tsan gin jrr	餐巾纸
order	diǎn cài	dien tsai	点菜
pepper	làjiāo	lah jiao	辣椒
pepper oil	làjiāo yóu	lah jiao you	辣椒油
plate	pánzi	pan dzz	盘子
restaurant	fànguǎnr	fan gwan	饭馆儿
roast	kǎo	kao	烤
salty	xián	shien	咸
sesame oil	xiāngyóu	shiang you	香油
Shanghai restaurant	Shànghǎiguǎnr	shang hai gwan	上海馆儿
Sichuan restaurant	Sìchuānguǎnr	sse chwan gwan	四川馆儿
soft drinks	ruǎn yǐnliào	ruan yin liao	软饮料
sour	suān	swen	酸
soy sauce	jiàngyóu	jiang you	酱油
spoon	sháozi	shao dzz	勺子
steam	zhēng	jren	蒸
stir fry	chǎo	chao	炒
sweet	tián	tien	甜

English translation	Pinyin	Pronunciation	Chinese
tea	*chá*	chah	茶
teacup	*chábēi*	chah bay	茶杯
toothpicks	*yáqiān*	yah chien	牙签
vinegar	*cù*	tsoo	醋
waiter	*fúwùyuán*	foo woo yuan	服务员
waitress	*nǚ fúfùyuán*	nui foo woo yuan	女服务员
Western food	*xī cān*	shee tsan	西餐
Western restaurant	*xīcānguǎnr*	shee tsan gwan	西餐馆儿
whisky	*wēishìjì*	way shrr jee	威士忌
wine	*pútao jiǔ*	poo tao geo	葡萄酒
Where is the dining room?	*cāntīng zài nǎli*	tsan ting dzai nah lee	餐厅在哪里？
Where can I find a good restaurant?	*nǎli yǒu hǎo de fànguǎnr*	nah lee you hao de fan gwan	哪里有好的饭馆儿？
Where can we get Peking Duck?	*nǎli kěyǐ chī dào Běijīng kǎoyā*	nah lee kuh yee chr dao bay jing kao yah	哪里可以吃到北京烤鸭？
Where shall we sit?	*wǒmen zuò zài nǎli*	wo men dzwo dzai nah lee	我们坐在哪里？
We have a party of four.	*wǒmen yígòng sì gè rén*	wo men yee goong sse guh ren	我们一共四个人。

English translation	Pinyin	Pronunciation	Chinese
party of five	wǔ gè rén	woo guh ren	五个人
party of eight	bā gè rén	bah guh ren	八个人
Do you have a menu in English?	yǒu yīngwén càidān ma	you ying wen tsai dan ma	有英文菜单吗？
What dishes would you recommend?	nǐ néng tuījiàn jǐ gè hǎo cài ma	nee neng twei jien gee guh hao tsai ma	你能推荐几个好菜吗？
What is your specialty?	nǐmen yǒu shénme tèbié de fēngwèi cài	nee men you shen ma te bie de feng way tsai	你们有什么特别的风味菜？
May I order now?	wǒ kěyǐ diǎn cài le ma	wo kuh yee dien tsai le ma	我可以点菜了吗？
Is there a restroom here?	zhèlǐ yǒu xǐshǒujiān ma	jre lee you shee shou jien ma	这里有洗手间吗？
Please give me	qǐng gěi wǒ	ching gay wo	请给我
a bottle of wine	yìpíng pútaojiǔ	yee ping poo tao geo	一瓶葡萄酒。
a bottle of beer	yì píng píjiǔ	yee ping pee geo	一瓶啤酒
a cup of tea	yì bēi chá	yee bay chah	一杯茶
a glass of ice water	yì bēi bīngshuǐ	yee bay bing shui	一杯冰水
I am a vegetarian.	wǒ zhǐ chī sù	wo jrr chr sue	我只吃素。
It is delicious.	hěn hǎo chī	hen hao chr	很好吃。

English translation	Pinyin	Pronunciation	Chinese
It's too hot.	*tài là le*	tai lah le	太辣了
too salty	*tài xián le*	tai shien le	太咸了
too sweet	*tài tián le*	tai tien le	太甜了
I did not order this dish.	*zhè bú shì wǒ diǎn de*	jre boo shr wo dien de	这不是我点的。
What's the name of that dish?	*nà gè cài jiào shénme*	nah guh tsai jiao shen ma	那个菜叫什么？
Please have some tea.	*qǐng hē chá*	ching huh chah	请喝茶。
I've had enough.	*gòu le*	goh le	够了。
May I have the check please?	*qǐng suàn zhàng*	ching swen jrang	请算账。

Food

beef	*niúròu*	niu row	牛肉
boild eggs	*zhǔ jīdàn*	jroo jee dan	煮鸡蛋
boiled dumpling	*shuǐ jiǎo*	shui jiao	水饺
bread	*miànbāo*	mien bao	面包
chicken	*jī*	jee	鸡
duck	*yā*	yah	鸭

English translation	*Pinyin*	Pronunciation	Chinese
dumpling	*jiǎozi*	jiao dzz	饺子
eggs	*jīdàn*	jee dan	鸡蛋
fried dumpling	*guō tiē*	gwo tieh	锅帖
fried eggs	*jiān jīdàn*	jien jee dan	煎鸡蛋
ham	*huǒ tuǐ*	huo tui	火腿
meat	*ròu*	row	肉
mutton	*yángròu*	yang row	羊肉
noodles in soup	*tāngmiàn*	tang mien	汤面
noodles	*miàntiáo*	mien tiao	面条
porridge	*zhōu*	jroh	粥
rice	*mǐfàn*	mee fan	米饭
scrambled eggs	*chǎo jīdàn*	chao jee dan	炒鸡蛋
steamed buns	*mántou*	man tow	馒头
steamed dumpling	*zhēn jiǎo*	jren jiao	蒸饺
steamed rolls	*huājuǎn*	hua juen	花卷
toast	*kǎo miànbāo*	kao mien bao	烤面包

Sea Food

carp	lǐyú	lee yu	鲤鱼
crab	*xiè*	shieh	蟹

English translation	*Pinyin*	Pronunciation	Chinese
fish	*yú*	yu	鱼
lobster	*lóng xiā*	long shiah	龙虾
mackeral	*qīngyú*	ching yu	鲭鱼
shrimp	*xiā*	shiah	虾
squid	*yóuyú*	you yu	鱿鱼
sturgeon	*huángyú*	huang yu	黄鱼

Vegetables

bamboo shoots	*sǔn*	suen	笋
bean curd	*dòufu*	doh foo	豆腐
bean sprouts	*dòuyá*	doh ya	豆芽
beans	*biǎndòu*	bien doh	扁豆
bitter melon	*kǔguā*	koo gwah	苦瓜
cabbage	*báicài*	bai tsai	白菜
carrots	*húluóbo*	hoo luo bo	胡萝卜
celery	*qíncài*	chin tsai	芹菜
corriander	*xiāngcài*	shiang tsai	香菜
cucumber	*huángguā*	huang gwah	黄瓜
eggplant	*qiézi*	chieh dzz	茄子
green pepper	*qīngjiāo*	ching jiao	青椒

English translation	*Pinyin*	Pronunciation	Chinese
lettuce	*shēngcài*	sheng tsai	生菜
lotus root	*ǒu*	oh	藕
mushrooms	*mógu*	maw goo	蘑菇
peas	*wāndòu*	wan doh	豌豆
spinach	*bōcài*	baw tsai	菠菜
tomato	*xīhóngshì*	shee hong shrr	西红柿
vegetable	*shūcài*	shoe tsai	蔬菜

Fruits

apple	*píngguǒ*	ping gwo	苹果
apricot	*xìngzi*	shing dzz	杏子
banana	*xiāngjiāo*	shiang jiao	香蕉
cherries	*yīngtáo*	ying tao	樱桃
chestnut	*lìzi*	lee dzz	栗子
coconut	*yēzi*	yeh dzz	椰子
dates	*zǎozi*	dzao dzz	枣子
fruit	*shuǐguǒ*	shui gwo	水果
grapes	*pútao*	poo tao	葡萄
lemon	*níngméng*	ning meng	柠檬
lichee	*lìzhī*	lee jrr	荔枝

English translation	Pinyin	Pronunciation	Chinese
longon	*lóngyǎn*	long yan	龙眼
mango	*mángguǒ*	mang gwo	芒果
orange	*júzi*	ju dzz	橘子
peach	*táozi*	tao dzz	桃子
pear	*lízi*	lee dzz	梨子
persimmon	*shìzi*	shrr dzz	柿子
pineapple	*bōluó*	baw law	菠萝
plums	*lǐzi*	lee dzz	李子
prunes	*méizi*	may dzz	梅子
strawberry	*cǎoméi*	tsao may	草莓
walnuts	*hétao*	huh tao	核桃
watermelon	*xīguā*	shee gwah	西瓜

Chinese Dishes to Try

1. Appetizers

braised bamboo shoots	*yóu mèn sǔn*	you men swen	油焖笋
cold platter	*lěngpán*	leng pan	冷盘

English translation	Pinyin	Pronunciation	Chinese
hot pickled cabbage	*là báicài*	lah bye tsai	辣白菜
jellyfish	*hǎizhépí*	hai jre pee	海蛰皮
marinated beef	*jiàng niúròu*	jiang new row	酱牛肉
preserved duck eggs	*sōnghuādàn*	soong hwa dan	松花蛋

2. Meat Dishes

diced pork with hot pepper	*gōng bǎo ròu dīng*	goong bow row ding	宫宝肉丁
meatballs of minced pork	*shīzi tóu*	shr dzz tow	狮子头
spicy shredded pork	*yú xiāng ròusī*	yu shiang row sse	鱼香肉丝
sweet & sour boneless pork	*táng cù lǐji*	tang tsoo lee jee	糖醋里脊
beef with oyster sauce	*háoyóu niúròu*	hao you new row	蚝油牛肉
shredded beef with peppers	*qīngjiāo niúròu*	ching jiao new row	青荽牛肉

English translation	Pinyin	Pronunciation	Chinese
sliced beef with asparagus	*lóng xū niúròu*	long shu new row	龙须牛肉
quick fried lamb with scallions	*cōng bào yángròu*	tsoong bow yang row	葱爆羊肉

3. Poultry

cold chicken with spicy sesame	*bàng bàng jī*	bang bang jee	棒棒鸡
crispy-skin chicken	*cuì pí jī*	tswei pee jee	脆皮鸡
deep fried chicken with walnuts	*hétao zhá jīpiàn*	huh tao jrah jee pien	核桃炸鸡片
diced chicken with cashew nuts	*yāoguǒ jī*	yao gwo jee	腰果鸡
strange-flavored chicken	*guài wèi jī*	gwai way jee	怪味鸡
camphor & tea smoked duck	*zhāng chá yā*	jrang chah yah	樟茶鸭
crispy duck	*xiāng sū yā*	shiang soo yah	香酥鸭
deep-fried pigeon	*zhá gēzi*	jrah guh dzz	炸鸽子

English translation	*Pinyin*	Pronunciation	Chinese
4. Seafood			
deep-fried fish balls	*zhá yú qiú*	jrah yu chew	炸鱼球
steamed whole fish	*qīng zhēng yú*	ching jreng yu	清蒸鱼
West Lake crispy fish	*xīhú cuì yú*	shee hoo tsui yu	西湖脆鱼
yellow croaker with pine nuts	*sōngzǐ huángyú*	soong dzz hwang yu	松子黄鱼
sauteed prawns	*qīng chǎo xiārén*	ching chao shiah ren	清炒虾仁
shrimp with hot peppers	*gōng bǎo xiārén*	goong bow shiah ren	宫宝虾仁
crabmeat with bean curd	*xiè ròu dòufu*	shieh row doh foo	蟹肉豆腐
5. Vegetables			
bean curd in casserole	*shāguō dòufu*	shah gwo doh foo	砂锅豆腐
bean curd with minced pork in hot sauce	*má pó dòufu*	mah paw doh foo	麻婆豆腐

English translation	Pinyin	Pronunciation	Chinese
broccoli in oyster sauce	*háoyóu jièlán*	hao you jieh lan	蚝油芥兰
Buddha's vegetable dish	*luó hàn zhāi*	lwo han jrai	罗汉斋
Chinese cabbage in cream sauce	*nǎiyóu báicài*	nai you bai tsai	奶油白菜
sauteed black mushrooms and bamboo shoots	*yùlánpiàn dōnggū*	yu lan pien doong goo	玉兰片冬菇
sauteed string beans	*gān biān sìjìdòu*	gang bien sse jee doh	干煸四季豆

6. Soup

English translation	Pinyin	Pronunciation	Chinese
bean curd & vegetable soup	*qīngcài dòufu tāng*	ching tsai doh foo town	青菜豆腐汤
hot & sour soup	*suān là tāng*	suan lah town	酸辣汤
sharkx fin soup	*yúchì tāng*	yu chr town	鱼翅汤
spicy vegetable soup	*zhàcài tāng*	jrah tsai town	榨菜汤
winter melon soup	*dōngguā tāng*	doong gwah town	冬瓜汤

English translation	*Pinyin*	Pronunciation	Chinese

7. Local Specialties

Mongolian BBQ	*Ménggǔ kǎoròu*	meng goo kao row	蒙古烤肉
Mongolian Hot Pot	*shuàn yángròu*	shwan yang row	涮羊肉
Peking Duck	*Běijīng kǎoyā*	bay jing kao yah	北京烤鸭

8. Desserts

almond gelatin	*xìngrén dòufu*	shing ren doh foo	杏仁豆腐
eight-treasured rice	*bā bǎo fàn*	bah bow fan	八宝饭
hot candied apple	*básī píngguǒ*	bah sse ping gwo	拔丝苹果
sesame cream	*zhīma hú*	jrr mah hoo	芝麻糊

9. Dim Sum

shrimp dumplings	*xiā jiǎo*	shiah jiao	虾饺
small steamed pork buns	xiǎo lóng bāo	shiao long bow	小笼包
spring rolls	*chūn juǎn*	chun juen	春卷
steamed pork dumpling	shāo mài	shao my	烧麦

English translation	Pinyin	Pronunciation	Chinese
steamed roast pork bun	*chá shāo bāo*	chah shao bow	茶烧包
sweet bean buns	*dòu shā bāo*	doh shah bow	豆砂包
sweet rice with meat stuffing in lotus leaves	*nuòmǐ zòngzi*	nuo mee dzong dzz	糯米粽子
turnip cake	*luóbo gāo*	luo bo gao	萝卜糕
wontons	*húntun*	hwen tuen	馄吞

Shopping

A few years back, tourists to China would be advised to take all their daily necessities with them, from personal hygiene products to toilet paper. Not any more. Today almost all that is necessary in one's everyday life is available in China. Unless you really prefer a certain brand, you don't have to be too concerned about leaving things behind.

Apart from daily necessities, there are plenty of souvenir items in China. High quality souvenirs are available in arts and crafts stores and friendship stores in big cities like Beijing and Shanghai. The price is normally moderate considering the higher value of the dollar against RMB, the Chinese currency. In many major tourist spots, foreign tourists may often find themselves in the middle of several Chinese peddlars speaking pidgin English and trying to sell them local souvenirs, often of inferior quality.

The amount of souvenirs is enormous, ranging from porcelain to jewelry, from calligraphy to antiques. A list of the major items in several big cities are listed in this phrase book. Also included here are some of the common words and phrases related to shopping.

English translation	Pinyin	Pronunciation	Chinese

General Terms

English translation	Pinyin	Pronunciation	Chinese
abacus	*suànpan*	swen pan	算盘
antique shop	*gǔdǒngdiàn*	goo doong dien	古董店
batik	*là rǎn*	lah ran	蜡染
bookstore	*shūdiàn*	shoo dien	书店
bracelet	*shǒuzhuó*	shou jruo	手镯
camera	*zhàoxiàngjī*	jrao shiang gee	照相机
carpet	*dìtǎn*	dee tan	地毯
carved lacquer	*diāoqī*	diao chee	雕漆
carvings	*diāokè*	diao keh	雕刻
cheap	*piányi*	pien yee	便宜
Chinese brush	*máobǐ*	mao bee	毛笔
Chinese painting	*Zhōngguó huà*	jrong gwo hua	中国画
cloisonne	*jǐngtàilán*	jing tai lan	景泰兰
close	*guān mén*	gwan men	关门
department store	*bǎi huò shāngdiàn*	bye hwo shang dien	百货商店
dinner-set	*cānjù*	tsan jui	餐具
embroidered table cloth	*xiù huā zhuōbù*	show hwa jrwo boo	绣花桌布

English translation	Pinyin	Pronunciation	Chinese
expensive	*guì*	gwei	贵
film	*jiāojuǎn*	jiao juan	胶卷
flower and bird	*huāniǎo*	hua niao	花鸟
free market	*zìyóu shìchǎng*	dzz you shrr chang	自由市场
friendship store	*yǒuyì shāngdiàn*	you yee shang dien	友谊商店
jade	*yù*	yu	玉
jadestone	*yù shí*	yu shrr	玉石
jewelry case	*shǒushì hé*	shou shrr heh	首饰盒
jewelry	*zhūbǎo*	droo bow	珠宝
lacquerware	*qīqì*	chee chee	漆器
landscape	*fēngjǐng*	feng jing	风景
lens	*jìngtóu*	jing toe	镜头
local specialty	*tèchǎn*	teh chan	特产
murals	*bì huà*	bee hua	壁画
music cassette	*yīnyuè cídài*	yin yueh tss dye	音乐磁带
open	*kāi mén*	kai men	开门
papercut	*jiǎnzhǐ*	jian jrr	剪纸
porcelain	*táoqì*	tao chee	陶器
ring	*jièzhi*	jieh jrr	戒指
shopping	*gòuwù*	goh woo	购物
signet	*yìnzhāng*	yin jrang	印章

English translation	*Pinyin*	Pronunciation	Chinese
souvenir	*jìniànpǐn*	jee nien pin	纪念品
souvenir shop	*jìniànpǐn diàn*	jee nien pin dien	纪念品店
tapestry	*guàtǎn*	gwah tan	挂毯
tea cup	*chá bēi*	chah bay	茶杯
tripod	*sānjiǎojià*	san jiao jiah	三角架
vase	*huāpíng*	hwa ping	花瓶
water color	*shuǐcǎi*	shui tsai	水彩
woodblock print	*mùbǎn shuǐyìn huà*	moo ban shui yin hua	木版水印画
Where is the department store?	*bǎihuò shāngdiàn zài nǎlǐ*	bye hwo shang dien dzai nah lee	百货商店在哪里？
I'd like to buy film.	*wǒ xiǎng mǎi yìjuǎn jiāojuǎn*	wo shiang my yee juen jiao juen	我想买一卷胶卷。
How much does it cost?	*duōshǎo qián*	dwo shao chien	多少钱？
Please show me the camera.	*qǐng bǎ zhàoxiàngjī gěi wǒ kànkan*	ching bah jrao shiang jee gay wo kan kan	请把照相机给我看看。
Can I try it?	*wǒ kěyǐ shìshi ma*	wo keh yee shr shr ma	我可以试试吗？
Can I exhange this?	*néng huàn yígè ma*	neng hwan yee guh ma	能换一个吗？

English translation	Pinyin	Pronunciation	Chinese
It's too expensive.	*tài guì le*	tai gwei le	太贵了。
Is your price firm?	*néng dǎ zhékòu ma*	neng dah jreh kou ma	能打折扣吗？

Toiletries

comb	*shūzi*	shoo dzz	梳子
conditioner	*hù fà sù*	hwo fah soo	护发素
lipstick	*kǒuhóng*	kou hong	口红
mirror	*jìngzi*	jing dzz	镜子
perfume	*xiāngshuǐ*	shiang shui	香水
shampoo	*xiāngbō*	shiang baw	香波
soap	*féizào*	fay dzao	肥皂
toiletries	*huàzhuāngpǐn*	hwah jruang pin	化妆品
toothbrush	*yáshuā*	yah shwah	牙刷
toothpaste	*yágāo*	yah gao	牙膏

Clothing

blouse	*nǚ chènshān*	nui chen shan	女衬衫
boots	*xuēzi*	shueh dzz	靴子
bra	*xiōngzhào*	shiong jrao	胸罩

English translation	Pinyin	Pronunciation	Chinese
brocade	*zhījǐnduàn*	jrr jin dwan	织锦缎
cap	*màozi*	mao dzz	帽子
cashmere	*kāisīmǐ*	kai sse mee	开司米
cloth	*bù*	boo	布
clothes	*yīfu*	yee foo	衣服
coat	*dàyī*	dah yee	大衣
fur/leather	*pí huò*	pee hwo	皮货
gloves	*shǒutào*	shou tao	手套
hankerchief	*shǒujuàn*	shou juen	手绢
pants	*kùzi*	koo dzz	裤子
pure wool	*chún yángmáo*	chun yang mao	纯羊毛
sandals	*liángxié*	liang shieh	凉鞋
satin	*duànzi*	dwan dzz	缎子
scarf	*wéijīn*	way jin	围巾
shirt	*chènshān*	chen shan	衬衫
shoes	*xié*	shieh	鞋
skirt	*qúnzi*	chuen dzz	裙子
slippers	*tuōxié*	tuo shieh	拖鞋
stockings	*chángtǒngwà*	chang tong wah	长统袜
suit	*tàofú*	tao foo	套服
sweater	*máoyī*	mao yee	毛衣

English translation	Pinyin	Pronunciation	Chinese
The Mao Suit	*Zhōngshān zhuāng*	jrong shan jruang	中山装
underwear	*nèikù*	nay koo	内裤
This shirt is too tight.	*zhèi jiàn chènshān tài jǐn le*	jreh jien chen shan tai jin le	这件衬衫太紧了。
That one is loose.	*nà yíjiàn hěn sōng*	nah yee jien hen soong	那一件很松。

Colors

black	*hē sè*	hay seh	黑色
blue	*lán sè*	lan seh	蓝色
brown	*zōng sè*	dzoong seh	棕色
color	*yánsè*	yan seh	颜色
dark	*shēn*	shen	深
green	*lǜ sè*	lui seh	绿色
light	*qiǎn/dàn*	chien/dan	浅、淡
orange	*chéng sè*	cheng seh	橙色
pink	*fěnhóng sè*	fen hong seh	粉红色
purple	*zǐ sè*	dzz seh	紫色
red	*hóng sè*	hong seh	红色

English translation	*Pinyin*	Pronunciation	Chinese
white	*bái sè*	bye seh	白色
yellow	*huáng sè*	hwang seh	黄色

Major Regional Souvenirs

BEIJING
jade, cloissone, calligraphy, paintings, antiques, leather

SHANGHAI
silk fabrics, tea utensils, jewelry, embroidery, carpet, Chinese medicine

TIANJIN
carpet, clay figurines, wood carvings, kites

SUZHOU
two-sided embroidery, sandalwood fans, rubbings, gold and silver products

HANGZHOU
sandalwood fans, box-wood products, Long-jing Tea

NANJING
silk textiles, tea utensils, precious stones

WUXI
woven silk, ceramics, clay figurines

YANGZHOU
lacquerware, papercuts

GUANGZHOU
inkstone, Chinese medicine

CHANGSHA
porcelain, stone earrings, embroidery

GUILIN
ink painting, bamboo and wickerwood products

KUNMING
copper products, embroidery

CHENGDU
silver products, pottery, embroidery

XIAN
stone rubbings, writing brush and ink, ink stone, wall hanging,
replica of ancient potter and ceramic figure

LANZHOU
    night-light cups, woven camel hair products

LUOYANG
    ceramics, lamps

QINGDAO
    beer, wine, shell products

CHANGCHUN
    marble carvings, quill painting

Entertainment

Peking Opera, perhaps the most well-known theatrical form among foreigners, is on the itinerary of most tour groups to China. Although the plot is often very hard to comprehend, the sumptuous costumes, the make-up and the acrobatics in many plays are always rather entertaining to foreign eyes.

Despite the established status of Peking Opera abroad, it is only one of the dozens of local operas in China. With plots based on ancient stories, most of these operas are hardly patronized by young viewers any more.

As in other countries, young people in China are more fond of the modern forms of entertainment, such as pop music. Karaoke bars, for example, are a favorite place for many young people to spend their evenings, although the price is outrageous, even for American standard. If a taxi driver offers to take you to a Karaoke bar and to give you a coke, just say no. That bottle of coke might well cost you a fortune. If you really want to go to a Karaoke bar without being ripped off, go with a Chinese who knows the situation very well.

English translation	*Pinyin*	Pronunciation	Chinese

Theater and Night Life

English translation	*Pinyin*	Pronunciation	Chinese
actor	*nán yǎnyuán*	nan yan yuen	男演员
actress	*nǚ yǎnyuán*	nui yan yuen	女演员
cartoon	*dònghuàpiān*	doong hwa pien	动画片
cinema	*diànyǐngyuàn*	dien ying yuen	电影院
circus	*mǎxì*	mah shee	马戏
classical music	*gǔdiǎn yīnyuè*	goo dien yin yueh	古典音乐
composer	*zuòqǔjiā*	dzwo chu giah	作曲家
concert hall	*yīnyuètīng*	yin yueh ting	音乐厅
concert	*yīnyuèhuì*	yin yueh hui	音乐会
conductor	*zhǐhuī*	jrr hui	指挥
documentary	*jìlùpiān*	jee loo pien	记录片
drama	*xìjù*	shee jui	戏剧
feature film	*gùshìpiān*	goo shr pien	故事片
folk music	*mínyuè*	min yueh	民乐
front seat	*qiánpái zuòwèi*	chien pai dzwo way	前排座位
intermission	*xiūxi*	show shee	休息
karaoke	*kǎ lā ōu kèi*	kah lah oh kay	卡拉ＯＫ
local opera	*dìfāngxì*	dee fang shee	地方戏

English translation	Pinyin	Pronunciation	Chinese
magic show	*móshù*	maw shoo	魔术
movie	*diànyǐng*	dien ying	电影
movie festival	*diànyǐngjié*	dien ying jieh	电影节
musical instrument	*yuèqì*	yueh chee	乐器
night life	*yè shēnghuó*	yeh sheng hwo	夜生活
Peking Opera	*Jīngjù*	jing ju	京剧
performance	*yǎnchū*	yan choo	演出
program	*jiémùdān*	jieh moo dan	节目单
puppet theater	*mù'ǒuxì*	moo oh shee	木偶戏
screen	*yínmù*	yin moo	银幕
sing a song	*chànggē*	chang geh	唱歌
song and dance	*gē wǔ*	geh woo	歌舞
symphony	*jiāoxiǎngyuè*	jiao shiang yueh	交响乐

I would like to see a movie.	*wǒ xiǎng kàn yìchǎng diànyǐng*	wo shiang kan yee chang dien ying	我想看一场电影。
I am interested in Peking Opera.	*wǒ duì jīngjù hěn yǒu xìngqù*	wo dui jing ju hen you shing chu	我对京剧很有兴趣。
Please give me a program.	*qǐng gěi wǒ yìzhāng jiémùdān*	ching gay wo yee jrang jieh moo dan	请给我一张节目单。

English translation	Pinyin	Pronunciation	Chinese
I like Chinese folk music.	*wǒ xǐhuān Zhōngguó mínjiān yīnyuè*	wo shee huan jrong gwo min jien yin yueh	我喜欢中国民间音乐。
May I record it?	*wǒ kěyǐ lùyīn ma*	wo keh yee loo yin mah	我可以录音吗？

Sports

acrobatics	*zájì*	dzah jee	杂技
badminton	*yǔmáoqiú*	yu mao chew	羽毛球
ball	*qiú*	chew	球
baseball	*bàngqiú*	bang chew	棒球
basketball	*lánqiú*	lan chew	篮球
gymnasium	*tǐyùguǎn*	tee yu gwan	体育馆
gymnastics	*tǐcāo*	tee tsao	体操
martial arts	*wǔshù*	woo shoo	武术
referee	*cáipàn*	tsai pan	裁判
soccer	*zúqiú*	dzoo chew	足球
sports	*tǐyù*	tee yu	体育
swimming	*yóuyǒng*	you yong	游泳
table tennis	*pīngpāngqiú*	ping pang chew	乒乓球
tennis	*wǎngqiú*	wang chew	网球

English translation	*Pinyin*	Pronunciation	Chinese
to lose	*shū*	shoo	输
to win	*yíng*	ying	赢
volleyball	*páiqiú*	pai chew	排球

Health

China has a rather complete medical care system. Besides full-fledged hospitals, most work places and major hotels have their own clinics and resident doctors to take care of minor ailments and administer first aid.

In some major Chinese cities, there are hospitals especially designed to treat foreign visitors. Experienced doctors trained in Western medicine are assigned to work there. Some of them can speak fluent English. But you cannot count on that. It is advisable that you bring an interpreter with you.

Today most Chinese hospitals practice both Chinese and Western medicine. The combination of the two has proven to be an effective way of treating many medical problems. Traditional Chinese medicine has been accepted by more and more Westerners as well. Acupuncture, for example, has gained popularity in the United States in recent years.

This section lists some of the most common medical terms as well as phrases you may need to use in case you need to see a doctor.

At the Hospital

English translation	*Pinyin*	Pronunciation	Chinese
acupuncture	*zhēnjiū*	jren jew	针灸
acute disease	*jíxìngbìng*	jee shing bing	急性病
ambulance	*jiùhùchē*	geo hoo che	救护车
appendicitis	*lánwěiyán*	lan way yan	阑尾炎
arthritis	*guānjiéyán*	gwan jieh yan	关节炎
bandage	*bēngdài*	beng dai	绷带
bleeding	*liúxiě*	lew shueh	流血
blood pressure	*xuèyā*	shueh yah	血压
bronchitis	*zhīqìguǎnyán*	jrr chee gwan yan	支气管炎
burn	*shāoshāng*	shao shang	烧伤
Chinese medicine	*zhōngyào*	jrong yao	中药
chronic disease	*mànxìngbìng*	man shing bing	慢性病
clinic	*zhěnsuǒ*	jren swo	诊所
constipation	*biànbì*	bien bee	便秘
cough	*késou*	keh soh	咳嗽
cramp	*chōujīn*	chow jin	抽筋
dentist	*yá yī*	yah yee	牙医
dept. of gynaecology	*fùkē*	foo kuh	妇科

English translation	Pinyin	Pronunciation	Chinese
dept. of orthopedics	*gŭkē*	goo kuh	骨科
dept. of pediatrics	*érkē*	er kuh	儿科
dept. of surgery	*wàikē*	wai kuh	外科
diabetes	*tángniàobìng*	tang niao bing	糖尿病
diagnose	*zhěnduàn*	jren duan	诊断
diarrhea	*lā dùzi*	lah doo dzz	拉肚子
doctor	*yīshēng*	yee sheng	医生
dysentery	*lìji*	lee jee	痢疾
electro-cardiograph	*xīndiàntú*	shin dien too	心电图
extract a tooth	*bá yá*	bah yah	拔牙
fever	*fāshāo*	fah shao	发烧
fill a tooth	*bŭ yá*	boo yah	补牙
gastritis	*wèiyán*	way yan	胃炎
headache	*tóu téng*	tow teng	头疼
heart disease	*xīnzàngbìng*	shin dzang bing	心脏病
hepatitis	*gānyán*	gan yan	肝炎
hospital	*yīyuàn*	yee yuen	医院
infection	*gănrăn*	gan ran	感染
injection	*dăzhēn*	dah jren	打针
injection room	*zhùshèshì*	jroo sheh shr	注射室

English translation	Pinyin	Pronunciation	Chinese
internal medicine	*nèikē*	nay kuh	内科
itch	*yǎng*	yang	痒
laboratory	*huàyànshì*	hwah yan shr	化验室
nurse	*hùshi*	hoo shr	护士
operation	*shǒushù*	shou shoo	手术
pain	*téng*	teng	疼
pharmacy	*qǔyàochù*	chu yao choo	取药处
pill	*yàowán*	yao wan	药丸
pneumonia	*fèiyán*	fay yan	肺炎
prescription	*yàofāng*	yao fang	药方
pulse	*màibó*	my baw	脉膊
registration office	*guàhàochù*	gwah hao choo	挂号处
rheumatism	*fēngshī*	feng shr	风湿
runny nose	*liú bíti*	lew bee tee	流鼻涕
sore throat	*hóulong téng*	hoh long teng	喉咙疼
stomach ache	*dùzi téng*	doo dzz teng	肚子疼
surgeon	*wàikē yīshēng*	wai kuh yee sheng	外科医生
tooth ache	*yá téng*	yah teng	牙疼
tuberculosis	*fèijiéhé*	fay jieh huh	肺结核
ultrasonic wave	*chāoshēngbō*	chao sheng baw	超声波
vomiting	*ǒu tù*	oh too	呕吐

English translation	*Pinyin*	Pronunciation	Chinese
Western medicine	*xīyào*	shee yao	西药
x-ray	*tòushì*	tow shr	透视
I don't feel well.	*wǒ bù shūfu*	wo boo shoo foo	我不舒服。
I have a fever.	*wǒ fāshāo le*	wo fah shao le	我发烧了。
I feel dizzy.	*wǒ yǒu xiē tóuyūn*	wo you shieh tow yun	我有些头晕。
I need to see a doctor.	*wǒ yào kàn yīshēng*	wo yao kan yee sheng	我要看医生。
Please hurry.	*qǐng kuài yìdiǎn*	ching kwai yee dien	请快一点。
I have a heart condition.	*wǒ yǒu xīnzàngbìng*	wo you shin dzang bing	我有心脏病。
I am allergic to dust.	*wǒ duì huīchén guòmǐn*	wo dwei hui chen gwo min	我对灰尘过敏。
I feel better now.	*wǒ hǎo yìdiǎn le*	wo hao yee dien le	我好一点了。

Parts of the Body

ankle	*huáigǔ*	hwai goo	踝骨
appendix	*lánwěi*	lan way	阑尾
arm	*gēbo*	guh baw	胳膊
artery	*dòngmài*	dong my	动脉

English translation	Pinyin	Pronunciation	Chinese
back	*bèi*	bay	背
bladder	*pángguāng*	pang gwang	膀胱
breast	*rǔfáng*	roo fang	乳房
chest	*xiōng*	shiong	胸
chin	*xiàba*	shiah bah	下巴
ear	*ěrduo*	er dwo	耳朵
elbow	*gēbozhǒu*	guh baw jrou	胳膊肘
eye	*yǎnjing*	yan jing	眼睛
face	*liǎn*	lien	脸
finger	*shǒuzhǐ*	shou jrr	手指
foot	*jiǎo*	jiao	脚
forehead	*qián'é*	chien eh	前额
gums	*yáyín*	yah yin	牙龈
hand	*shǒu*	shou	手
head	*tóu*	tow	头
heart	*xīnzàng*	shin dzang	心脏
heel	*jiǎogēn*	jiao gen	脚根
hip	*túnbù*	tun boo	臀部
intestines	*chángzi*	chang dzz	肠子
kidney	*shèn*	shen	肾
knee	*xīgài*	shee guy	膝盖

English translation	*Pinyin*	Pronunciation	Chinese
leg	*tuǐ*	twei	腿
lips	*zuǐchún*	dzwei chun	嘴唇
liver	*gān*	gan	肝
lung	*fèi*	fay	肺
mouth	*zuǐ*	dzwei	嘴
neck	*bózi*	baw dzz	脖子
nerves	*shénjīng*	shen jing	神经
nose	*bízi*	bee dzz	鼻子
shoulder	*jiān*	jien	肩
skin	*pífu*	pee foo	皮肤
spine	*jízhù*	jee jroo	脊柱
throat	*hóulong*	hou long	喉咙
toe	*jiǎozhǐ*	jiao jrr	脚指
tonsils	*biǎntáoxiàn*	bien tao shien	扁桃腺
tooth	*yá*	yah	牙
wrist	*shǒuwàn*	shou wan	手腕

Pharmaceuticals

alcohol	*jiǔjīng*	geo jing	酒精
allergy pills	*guòmǐnyào*	gwo min yao	过敏药

English translation	*Pinyin*	Pronunciation	Chinese
antibiotic	*kàngshēngsù*	kang sheng soo	抗生素
antiseptic	*kàng jūn jì*	kang jrun jee	抗菌剂
aspirin	*āsīpílín*	ah sse pee lin	阿斯皮林
cough syrup	*zhǐ ké tángjiāng*	jrr kuh tang jiang	止咳糖浆
eyedrops	*yǎn yào*	yan yao	眼药
iodine	*diǎnjiǔ*	dien geo	碘酒
mercurochrome	*hóng gǒng*	hong goong	红汞
paragoric	*zhǐ téng jì*	jrr teng gee	止疼剂
sleeping pill	*ānmiányào*	an mien yao	安眠药
smelling salts	*tàn suān ān*	tan swan an	炭酸氨
thermometer	*tǐwēnbiǎo*	tee wen biao	体温表
tranquilizer	*āndìngyào*	an ding yao	安定药
vaseline	*fánshìlín*	fan shr lin	凡士林
vitamin	*wéishēngsù*	way sheng soo	维生素

Doing Business

For those who are on a business trip to China, this chapter offers some useful words and phrases. It is almost a cliche to say that doing business with China demands a lot of patience. Given the cultural differences between China and the United States, it is not easy to reach an agreement without long negotiations. To understand each other's stand and the different ways of doing things would help speed up business negotiations.

English translation	*Pinyin*	Pronunciation	Chinese
General Terms			
agreement	*xiéyì*	shieh yee	协议
assemble	*zǔzhuāng*	dzoo jruang	组装
business	*shēngyi*	sheng yee	生意
buy	*mǎijìn*	my jin	买进
capital	*zījīn*	dzz jin	资金
catalog	*mùlù*	moo loo	目录
cheap	*piányi*	pien yee	便宜

English translation	Pinyin	Pronunciation	Chinese
chemicals	*huàgōngpǐn*	hwa goong pin	化工品
customer	*kèhù*	kuh hoo	客户
economy	*jīngjì*	jing jee	经济
equipment	*shèbèi*	sheh bay	设备
expensive	*guì*	gwei	贵
export	*chūkǒu*	choo koh	出口
final offer	*zuìzhōngpán*	dzwei jrong pan	最终盘
firm offer	*shípán*	shr pan	实盘
foreign trade	*duìwài màoyì*	dwei wai mao yee	对外贸易
freight	*yùnfèi*	yun fay	运费
import	*jìnkǒu*	jin koh	进口
insurance	*bǎoxiǎn*	bow shien	保险
joint venture	*hézī qǐyè*	huh dzz chee yeh	合资企业
loan	*dàikuǎn*	dai kwan	贷款
loss	*sǔnshī*	swen shr	损失
market	*shìchǎng*	shr chang	市场
minerals	*kuàngchǎnpǐn*	kwang chan pin	矿产品
negotiation	*tánpàn*	tan pan	谈判
output	*chǎnliàng*	chan liang	产量
policy	*zhèngcè*	jreng tse	政策
price	*jiàgé*	jia guh	价格

English translation	Pinyin	Pronunciation	Chinese
price list	*jiàgédān*	jiah guh dan	价格单
product	*chǎnpǐn*	chan pin	产品
profit	*lìrùn*	lee run	利润
quote	*bàojià*	bow jiah	报价
sample	*yàngpǐn*	yang pin	样品
sell	*xiāoshòu*	shiao shou	销售
spare parts	*língjiàn*	ling jien	零件
style	*kuǎnshì*	kwan shr	款式
trade fair	*jiāoyìhuì*	jiao yee hui	交易会
trade	*màoyì*	mao yee	贸易

Useful Phrases

Can you give me a quote?	*nǐ néng gěi wǒ yígè bàojià ma*	nee neng gay wo yee guh bow jiah ma	你能给我一个报价吗？
Is this the CIF price?	*nǐ gěi de shì dào àn jià ma*	nee gay de shr dao an jiah ma	你给的是到岸价吗？
What are your terms and conditions?	*nǐmen de tiáojiàn shì shénme*	nee men de tiao jien shr shen ma	你们的条件是什么？
Our products have high quality.	*wǒmen de chǎnpǐn zhìliàng hěn gāo*	wo men de chan pin jrr liang hen gao	我们的产品质量很高。

English translation	Pinyin	Pronunciation	Chinese
When shall we sign the contract?	*wǒmen shénme shíhòu qiānyuē*	wo men shen me shr hoh chien yueh	我们什么时候签约？
We will order 100 pieces.	*wǒmen dìnggòu yìbǎi jiàn*	wo men ding goh yee bye jien	我们定购一百件。
Can you meet our requirement?	*nǐmen néng dá dào wǒmen de yāoqiú ma*	nee men neng dah dao wo men de yao chew ma	你们能达到我们的要求吗？
I'd like to talk about discounts.	*wǒ xiǎng tán yíxià zhékòu wèntí.*	wo shiang tan yee shiah jre koh wen tee	我想谈一下折扣问题。
How much commission do you give?	*nǐmen gěi duōshǎo yōngjīn*	nee men gay dwo shao yong jin	你们给多少佣金？
We don't allow any commission.	*wǒmen bù gěi yōngjīn*	wo men boo gay yong jin	我们不给佣金。
What are the payment terms?	*fùkuǎn tiáojiàn shì shénme*	foo kwan tiao jien shr shen ma	付款条件是什么？
I can provide a letter of credit.	*wǒ kěyǐ tígōng xìnyòngzhèng*	wo kuh yee tee goong shin yong jreng	我可以提供信用证。

Useful Addresses and Telephone Numbers

US Government Offices in China

Embassy
3 Xiushui Bei Jie
Jianguomenwai, Beijing 100600
Tel: (8610) 532-3831
FAX: Ambassador/Economic: (8610) 532-6422
Commercial: (8610) 532-3178
Visas: (8610) 532-3178

Chengdu Consulate General
4 Lingshiguan Lu
Chengdu, Sichuan Province 610042
Tel: (8628) 558-9642
FAX: (8628) 558-3520

Guangzhou Consulate General
1 Shamian Nan Jie
Guangzhou, Guangdong Province 510133
Tel: (8620) 888-8911
Fax: (8620) 886-2341

Shanghai Consulate General
1469 Huaihai Zhong Lu
Shanghai 200031
Tel: (8621) 433-6880
Fax: (8621) 433-4122, 433-1476

Shenyang Consulate General
No. 52, Shi Si Wei Lu
Heping District
Shenyang, Liaoning Province 110003
Tel: (8624) 282-0057
Fax: (8624) 282-0074

Hong Kong Consulate General
26 Garden Road
Hong Kong
Tel: (852) 2523-9011
Fax: (852) 2845-9800

PRC Government Offices in the US

Embassy
2300 Connecticut Avenue NW
Washington, DC 20008
Tel: (202) 328-2500, 328-2501, 328-2502
Fax: (202) 328-2582
Visas: (202) 328-2517   Fax: (202) 328-2564

Chicago Consulate General
100 W. Erie Street
Chicago, IL 60610
Visas: (312) 803-0098
Fax: (312) 803-0114

Houston Consulate General
3417 Montrose Boulevard
Houston, TX 77006
Visas: (713) 524-4311, 524-2304
Fax: (713) 524-7656

Los Angeles Consulate General
443 Shatto Place
Los Angeles, CA 90020
Visas: (213) 380-2506, 380-2507, 380-0372
Fax: (213) 380-1961

New York Consulate General
520 12th Avenue
New York, NY 10036
Visas: (212) 330-7410
Fax: (212) 502-0248

San Francisco Consulate General
1450 Laguna Street
San Francisco, CA 94115
Visas: (415) 563-4857, 563-9232
Fax: (415) 563-0494, 563-0131

Traveler's Dictionary

English	*Pinyin*	Chinese
a dozen	*yìdá*	一打
a few	*jǐgè*	几个
a million	*yìbǎiwàn*	一百万
a pair	*yìshuāng, yíduì, yífù*	一双，一对，一副
abacus	*suànpán*	算盘
about	*guānyú, dàyuē*	关于，大约
accept	*jiēshòu*	接受
accompany	*péitóng*	陪同
account	*zhànghù*	帐户
ache	*téng*	疼
acre	*yīngmǔ*	英亩
actor	*nán yǎnyuán*	男演员
actress	*nǚ yǎnyuán*	女演员
acupuncture	*zhēnjiǔ*	针灸
acute disease	*jíxìngbìng*	急性病
address	*dìzhǐ*	地址
addressee	*shōuxìnrén*	收信人
after	*yǐhòu*	以后
again	*zài*	再

English	*Pinyin*	Chinese
agreement	*xiéyì*	协议
air conditioner	*kōngtiáo*	空调
air letter, airmail	*hángkōngxìn*	航空信
airplane	*fēijī*	飞机
airport	*jīchǎng*	机场
alcohol	*jiǔjīng*	酒精
all right	*xíng*	行
allergic (to)	*guòmǐn*	过敏
allergy pills	*guòmǐnyào*	过敏药
alone	*dāndú*	单独
allow	*yǔnxǔ*	允许
alright	*hǎo, kěyǐ*	好，可以
also	*yě*	也
ambulance	*jiùhùchē*	救护车
American	*Měiguó rén*	美国人
ankle	*huáigǔ*	踝骨
answer	*huídá*	回答
antibiotic	*kàngshēngsù*	抗生素
antique shop	*gǔwán diàn*	古玩店
antiseptic	*kàngjūnjì*	抗菌剂
appendicitis	*lánwěiyán*	阑尾炎

English	Pinyin	Chinese
appendix	*lánwěi*	阑尾
apple	*píngguǒ*	苹果
apricot	*xìngzi*	杏子
April	*sìyuè*	四月
arm	*gēbo*	胳膊
art	*yìshù*	艺术
art school	*měishù xuéyuàn*	美术学院
artery	*dòngmài*	动脉
arthritis	*guānjiéyán*	关节炎
ashtray	*yānhuīgāng*	烟灰缸
aspirin	*āsīpílín*	阿司匹林
assemble	*zǔzhuāng*	组装
at	*zài*	在
at midday (noon)	*zhōngwǔ*	中午
at night	*yèli*	夜里
August	*bāyuè*	八月
Australian	*Àodàlìyà rén*	澳大利亚人
autumn	*qiūtiān*	秋天
back (behind, rear)	*hòu*	后
back (of body)	*bèi*	背
bad	*huài, bùhǎo*	坏，不好

English	*Pinyin*	Chinese
badminton	*yǔmáoqiú*	羽毛球
bag	*bāo*	包
baggage	*xíngli*	行李
ball	*qiú*	球
bamboo chopsticks	*zhú kuàizi*	竹筷子
bamboo shoots	*sǔn*	笋
bambooware	*zhúqì*	竹器
banana	*xiāngjiāo*	香蕉
bandage	*bēngdài*	绷带
bank	*yínháng*	银行
bank draft	*yínháng zhīpiào*	银行支票
Bank of China	*Zhōngguó yínháng*	中国银行
banker	*yínhángjiā*	银行家
barber shop	*lǐfàguǎn*	理发馆
basis	*jīchǔ*	基础
basketball	*lánqiú*	蓝球
bath (take a)	*xǐzǎo*	洗澡
batik	*làrǎn yìnhuābù*	蜡染印花布
battery	*diànchí*	电池
beans	*biǎndòu*	扁豆
bean curd	*dòufu*	豆腐

English	*Pinyin*	Chinese
bean sprouts	*dòuyár*	豆芽儿
beautiful	*měi, piàoliang*	美，漂亮
bed	*chuáng*	床
beef	*niúròu*	牛肉
beer	*píjiǔ*	啤酒
before	*yǐqián*	以前
behind schedule	*wǎndiǎn*	晚点
beige	*mǐsè (de)*	米色（的）
better	*hǎo yìdiǎn*	好一点
beverage	*yǐnliào*	饮料
bicycle	*zìxíngchē*	自行车
big	*dà*	大
bigger	*dà yìdiǎn*	大一点
bill (currency)	*zhǐbì*	纸币
bird	*niǎo*	鸟
birthday	*shēngri*	生日
biscuits	*bǐnggān*	饼干
bitter melon	*kǔguā*	苦瓜
black	*hēisè*	黑色
bladder	*pángguāng*	膀胱
blanket	*tǎnzi*	毯子

English	Pinyin	Chinese
bleeding	*liúxuè*	流血
blood pressure	*xuèyā*	血压
blouse	*nǚ chènshān*	女衬衫
blue	*lánsè*	蓝色
boarding card	*dēngjī pái*	登机牌
boat	*chuán*	船
boat ticket	*chuánpiào*	船票
boiled dumpling	*shuǐjiǎo*	水饺
boiled eggs	*zhǔ jīdàn*	煮鸡蛋
bonus	*jiǎngjīn*	奖金
bookstore	*shūdiàn*	书店
boots	*xuēzi*	靴子
boring	*wúliáo*	无聊
bottle	*píng*	瓶
bottoms up	*gānbēi*	干杯
bowel movement	*dàbiàn*	大便
bowels	*cháng*	肠
bowl	*wǎn*	碗
bra	*rǔzhào*	乳罩
bracelet	*shǒuzhuó*	手镯
brandy	*báilándì*	白兰地

English	*Pinyin*	Chinese
bread	*miànbāo*	面包
breakfast	*zǎofàn*	早饭
breast	*rǔfáng*	乳房
bridge	*qiáo*	桥
bright	*liàng*	亮
bring	*nálái*	拿来
British	*Yīngguó rén*	英国人
broadcasting station	*guǎngbōtái*	广播台
brocade	*zhījǐnduàn*	织锦缎
broil	*kǎo*	烤
bronchitis	*zhīqìguǎnyán*	支气管炎
brown	*kāfēi sè*	咖啡色
bubble gum	*kǒuxiāngtáng*	口香糖
burn	*shāoshāng*	烧伤
bus	*chē*	车
bus stop	*qìchē zhàn*	汽车站
business	*shēngyi*	生意
businessman	*shíyè jiā*	实业家
businesswoman	*nǔ shíyèjiā*	女实业家
buy	*mǎi, mǎijìn*	买，买进
cabbage	*báicài*	白菜

English	Pinyin	Chinese
cabin	*cāng*	舱
cadres	*gànbù*	干部
cafe	*kāfēi diàn*	咖啡店
call	*jiào*	叫
camera	*zhàoxiàngjī*	照相机
can (be able to)	*néng*	能
Canadian	*Jiānádà rén*	加拿大人
cancel	*qǔxiāo*	取消
candies	*táng*	糖
Cantonese restaurant	*Guǎngdōng fànguǎn*	广东饭馆
cap	*màozi*	帽子
capital (funds)	*zījīn*	资金
captain (skipper)	*chuánzhǎng*	船长
carp	*lǐyú*	鲤鱼
carpet	*dìtǎn*	地毯
carrots	*húluóbo*	胡萝卜
cartoons	*dònghuàpiàn*	动画片
carved lacquerware	*diāoqī*	雕漆
carvings	*diāokè*	雕刻
cash	*xiànjīn*	现金
cash a check	*duìxiàn zhīpiào*	兑现支票

English	*Pinyin*	Chinese
cashmere	*kāishìmǐ*	开士米
cassette	*héshìcídài*	盒式磁带
cat	*māo*	猫
catalog	*mùlù*	目录
catch a chill	*zhāoliáng*	着凉
catch a cold	*gǎnmào le*	感冒了
catty (a unit of weight)	*jīn*	斤
caution	*xiǎoxīn*	小心
cave	*shāndòng*	山洞
celery	*qíncài*	芹菜
change money	*duìhuàn*	兑换
cheap	*piányi*	便宜
check-in (out) counter	*jiǎnpiàochù*	检票处
cheers	*gānbēi*	干杯
chemicals	*huàgōngpǐn*	化工品
cherries	*yīngtáo*	樱桃
chest	*xiōng*	胸
chestnut	*lìzī*	栗子
chicken	*jī*	鸡
child	*háizi*	孩子
children	*háizimēn*	孩子们

English	Pinyin	Chinese
Children's Day (June 1)	*liùyī értóng jié*	六一儿童节
Children's Palace	*shàonián gōng*	少年宫
chili pepper (powder)	*làjiāo fěn*	辣椒粉
chin	*xiàba*	下巴
Chinese acrobatics	*Zhōngguó zájì*	中国杂技
Chinese brush	*máobǐ*	毛笔
Chinese cabbage	*dàbáicài*	大白菜
Chinese classical music	*Zhōngguó gǔdiǎn yīnyuè*	中国古典音乐
Chinese currency	*rénmínbì*	人民币
Chinese folk music	*Zhōngguó mínyuè*	中国民乐
Chinese food	*zhōngcān*	中餐
Chinese ink stick	*mò*	墨
Chinese medicine	*zhōngyào*	中药
Chinese musical instrument	*mínzúyuèqì*	民族乐器
Chinese New Year (Spring Festival)	*chūnjié*	春节
Chinese paintings	*Zhōngguó huà*	中国画
chocolate	*qiǎokèlì*	巧克力
chopsticks	*kuàizi*	筷子
chronic disease	*mànxìngbìng*	慢性病
chrysanthemum	*júhuā*	菊花

English	*Pinyin*	Chinese
church	*jiàotáng*	教堂
C.I.F. (cost, insurance & freight)	*dào'àn jiàgé*	到岸价格
cigar	*xuějiā*	雪茄
cigarettes	*xiāngyān*	香烟
cinema	*diànyǐngyuàn*	电影院
circus	*mǎxì*	马戏
city	*chéngshì*	城市
city map	*shìqū dìtú*	市区地图
classical music	*gǔdiǎn yīnyuè*	古典音乐
clean	*gānjìng*	干净
clear (weather)	*qíng*	晴
clearly	*qīngchǔ*	清楚
clinic	*zhěnliáosuǒ*	诊疗所
clock	*zhōng*	钟
cloisonne	*jǐngtàilán*	景泰蓝
close, closed	*guānmén*	关门
cloth	*bù*	布
cloth shoes	*bù xié*	布鞋
clothes	*yīfu*	衣服
clothing shop	*fúzhuāngdiàn*	服装店

English	*Pinyin*	Chinese
coat	*dàyī*	大衣
coconut	*yēzi*	椰子
coffee	*kāfēi*	咖啡
coffee-service	*kāfēijù*	咖啡具
coins	*yìngbì*	硬币
cold	*lěng*	冷
cold cream	*lěngshuāng*	冷霜
cold water	*liángshuǐ*	凉水
cold wave	*lěngtàng*	冷烫
color	*yánsè*	颜色
color film	*cǎisè jiāojuǎn*	彩色胶卷
comb	*shūzi*	梳子
come	*lái*	来
comic dialog	*xiàngsheng*	相声
commission	*yòngjīn*	佣金
compartment (on a train)	*chēxiāng*	车厢
complex	*fùzá*	复杂
compose	*zuòqǔ*	作曲
concert	*yīnyuèhuì*	音乐会
concert hall	*yīnyuètīng*	音乐厅
conclude	*dáchéng, jiéshù*	达成，结束

English	Pinyin	Chinese
conditions	*tiáojiàn*	条件
conductor (on a train)	*lièchēyuán*	列车员
constipation	*biànbì*	便秘
consultant	*gùwèn*	顾问
contagious disease	*chuánrǎnbìng*	传染病
continue	*jìxù*	继续
contract	*hétong, qìyuē*	合同，契约
cool	*liángkuai*	凉快
cooperate	*hézuò*	合作
correct	*duìde*	对的
corriander	*xiāngcài*	香菜
cost	*chéngběn*	成本
cough	*késòu*	咳嗽
cough drops	*késòu yào*	咳嗽药
cough syrup	*zhǐké tángjiāng*	止咳糖浆
countryside	*nóngcūn*	农村
county government	*xiànzhèngfǔ*	县政府
cow	*niú*	牛
crab	*pángxiè*	螃蟹
cramp	*chōujīn*	抽筋
credit card	*xìnyòngkǎ*	信用卡

English	*Pinyin*	Chinese
cucumber	*huángguā*	黄瓜
cup	*bēizi*	杯子
currency	*huòbì*	货币
cushion	*diànzi*	垫子
customer	*kèhù*	客户
customs	*hǎiguān*	海关
cuttle fish (squid)	*yóuyú*	鱿鱼
dance (*n*)	*wǔhuì*	舞会
danger, dangerous	*wēixiǎn*	危险
dark (color)	*shēn*	深
dark (dim)	*àn*	暗
dates (fruit)	*zǎozī*	枣子
day	*rì, tiān*	日，天
day after tomorrow	*hòutiān*	后天
daycare center	*tuō'érsuǒ*	托儿所
December	*shí'èryuè*	十二月
deck	*jiǎbǎn*	甲板
declare (at customs)	*bàoguān*	报关
deep (water)	*shēn*	深
deep-fry	*zhá*	炸
deer	*lù*	鹿

English	*Pinyin*	Chinese
degree	*dù*	度
delicious	*wèidàohěnhǎo*	味道很好
deluxe cabin	*tèděngcāng*	特等舱
dentist	*yákē yīshēng*	牙科医生
depart	*líkāi*	离开
department of dentistry	*yákē*	牙科
dept. of gynaecology	*fùkē*	妇科
dept. of internal medicine	*nèikē*	内科
dept. of orthopedics	*gǔkē*	骨科
department of pediatrics	*érkē*	儿科
department store	*bǎihuò shāngdiàn*	百货商店
department of surgery	*wàikē*	外科
departure (to leave)	*líkāi*	离开
deposit money	*cún qián*	存钱
develop	*fāzhǎn*	发展
diabetes	*tángniàobìng*	糖尿病
(be) diabetic	*tángniàobìngrén*	糖尿病人
diagnose	*zhěnduàn*	诊断
dial	*bō*	拨
diarrhea	*xièdù*	泻肚
diarrhea medicine	*zhǐxiè yào*	止泻药

English	*Pinyin*	Chinese
difficult	*nán*	难
dining car	*cānchē*	餐车
dining room	*cāntīng*	餐厅
dinner	*wǎnfàn*	晚饭
dinner service	*cānjù*	餐具
direction	*fāngxiàng*	方向
director	*dǎoyǎn*	导演
dirty	*zāng*	脏
discount	*zhékòu*	折扣
discuss	*tǎolùn, shāngtǎo*	讨论，商讨
dishes	*cài*	菜
dizzy	*tóuyūn*	头晕
dock	*mǎ tóu*	码头
doctor	*yīshēng*	医生
documentary films	*jìlùpiàn*	记录片
dog	*gǒu*	狗
donkey	*lú*	驴
don't touch	*qǐng wù chùmō*	请勿触摸
double room	*shuāngrén fángjiān*	双人房间
downstairs	*lóuxià*	楼下
Dragon Boat Festival	*Duānwǔjié*	端午节

English	*Pinyin*	Chinese
drink	*hē*	喝
drinking water	*yǐnyòngshuǐ*	饮用水
driver (taxi, bus)	*sījī*	司机
dry	*gānzào*	干燥
dry cleaning	*gānxǐ*	干洗
duck	*yā*	鸭
dumpling	*jiǎozi*	饺子
duty	*shuì*	税
dysentry	*lìji*	痢疾
ear	*ěrduo*	耳朵
early	*zǎo*	早
early morning	*qīngzǎo*	清早
east	*dōng*	东
easy	*róngyì*	容易
eat	*chī*	吃
economy	*jīngjì*	经济
editor	*biānjí*	编辑
eel	*mányú*	鳗鱼
egg (chicken)	*jīdàn*	鸡蛋
eggplant	*qiézi*	茄子
eiderdown	*yāróng*	鸭绒

English	*Pinyin*	Chinese
eight	*bā*	八
eighth	*dìbā*	第八
eight hundred	*bābǎi*	八百
eighteen	*shíbā*	十八
eighty	*bāshí*	八十
elbow	*gēbo*	胳膊
electric fan	*diànshàn*	电扇
electrocardiogram	*xīndiàntú*	心电图
elevator	*diàntī*	电梯
eleven	*shíyī*	十一
embroidered table cloth	*xiùhuā zhuōbù*	绣花桌布
emergency exit	*jǐnjí chūkǒu*	紧急出口
empty	*kōng*	空
endorse	*qiānmíng*	签名
engine room (on a ship)	*jīcāngjiān*	机舱间
engineer	*gōngchéngshī*	工程师
English	*Yīngwén*	英文
enjoyable	*yúkuài de*	愉快的
enough	*gòu le*	够了
enter	*jìnrù*	进入
entrance	*jìnkǒu, rùkǒu*	进口，入口

English	*Pinyin*	Chinese
envelopes	*xìnfēng*	信封
equipment	*shèbèi*	设备
exchange	*huàn*	换
exchange office	*duìhuàn chù*	兑换处
exchange rate	*duìhuànlù*	兑换率
exchange slip	*duìhuàndān*	兑换单
excluding meals	*huǒshí bù zài nèi*	伙食不在内
exhibit	*zhǎnpǐn*	展品
exit	*chūkǒu*	出口
expensive	*guì*	贵
export	*chūkǒu*	出口
express	*kuài xìn*	快信
extra blanket	*éwàide tǎnzì*	额外的毯子
extra pillow	*éwàide zhěntou*	额外的枕头
extract a tooth	*bá yá*	拔牙
extremely	*fēicháng*	非常
eye	*yǎnjing*	眼睛
eyedrops	*yǎnyào*	眼药
face	*liǎn*	脸
factory	*gōngchǎng*	工厂
factory manager	*chǎngzhǎng*	厂长

English	Pinyin	Chinese
false	*jiǎ*	假
far	*yuǎn*	远
farmer	*nóngmín*	农民
fast	*kuài*	快
faster	*kuài yì diǎn*	快一点
fat	*pàng*	胖
faucet	*lóngtóu*	龙头
feature film	*gùshi piàn*	故事片
February	*èryuè*	二月
feel	*gǎnjué*	感觉
fen	*fēn*	分
fever	*fāshāo*	发烧
few	*shǎo*	少
field	*tián, tǔdì*	田，土地
fifteen	*shíwǔ*	十五
fifth	*dìwú*	第五
fifty	*wǔshí*	五十
fill a tooth	*bǔ yá*	补牙
film festival	*diànyǐngjié*	电影节
film studios	*diànyǐng zhìpiānchǎng*	电影制片厂
final offer	*zuìzhōng pán*	最终盘

English	*Pinyin*	Chinese
fine	*hěnhǎo*	很好
finger	*shǒuzhǐ*	手指
finish	*wán le*	完了
firm offer	*shípán*	实盘
first	*xiān, dìyī*	先，第一
first-class (cabin)	*tóuděng (cāng)*	头等（舱）
fish	*yú*	鱼
five	*wǔ*	五
five hundred	*wǔbǎi*	五百
flight number	*hángbān hào*	航班号
floor	*dìbǎn*	地板
flower and bird	*huāniǎo*	花鸟
foggy	*yǒu wù*	有雾
folk music	*mínjiān yīnyuè*	民间音乐
food	*shíwù*	食物
foot (measurement)	*yīngchǐ*	英尺
foot (part of body)	*jiǎo*	脚
for rent	*chūzū*	出租
for sale	*dàishòu*	待售
forehead	*qián'é*	前额
foreign investment	*wàiguó tóuzī*	外国投资

English	*Pinyin*	Chinese
foreign lang. bookstore	*wàiwén shūdiàn*	外文书店
foreign trade	*wàimào*	外贸
foreman	*gōngzhǎng*	工长
fork	*chāzi*	叉子
form	*biǎogé*	表格
forty	*sìshí*	四十
four	*sì*	四
four hundred	*sìbǎi*	四百
fourteen	*shísì*	十四
fourth	*dìsì*	第四
fourth class (cabin)	*sì děng (cāng)*	四等（舱）
fox	*húli*	狐狸
free market	*zìyóu shìchǎng*	自由市场
freight	*yùnfèi*	运费
French	*Fǎwén*	法文
French francs	*fǎláng*	法郎
fresh	*xīnxiānde*	新鲜的
Friday	*xīngqīwǔ*	星期五
fried dumpling	*guōtiē*	锅贴
fried eggs	*jiānjīdàn*	煎鸡蛋
friend	*péngyou*	朋友

English	*Pinyin*	Chinese
friendship store	*yǒuyì shāngdiàn*	友谊商店
from	*cóng*	从
front	*qián*	前
front row	*qiánpái*	前排
frozen	*dòng de*	冻的
fruit	*shuǐguǒ*	水果
fry	*jiān*	煎
full	*mǎn, bǎo*	满，饱
fur	*pí, pízi*	皮，皮子
garlic	*suàn*	蒜
gastrits	*wèiyán*	胃炎
German (people)	*Déguó rén*	德国人
German (language)	*Déwén*	德文
get off	*xià chē*	下车
get on	*shàng chē*	上车
gift	*lǐpǐn*	礼品
ginger	*jiāng*	姜
give	*gěi*	给
glass	*bōlibēi*	玻璃杯
gloves	*shǒutào*	手套
glue	*jiāoshuǐ*	胶水

English	*Pinyin*	Chinese
go	*qù*	去
go ashore	*kào'àn*	靠岸
go with (accompany)	*péi*	陪
goldfish	*jīnyú*	金鱼
good	*hǎo*	好
good-bye	*zàijiàn*	再见
grapes	*pútao*	葡萄
green pepper	*qīngjiāo*	青椒
green tea	*lǜchá*	绿茶
grey squirrel	*huīshǔ*	灰鼠
group	*tuántǐ*	团体
guest house	*zhāodàisuǒ*	招待所
guide	*dǎoyóu*	导游
guide book	*lǚyóu zhǐnán*	旅游指南
gums	*yáyín*	牙龈
gymnasium	*tǐyùguǎn*	体育馆
gymnastic show	*tǐcāo biǎoyǎn*	体操表演
haircut	*lǐfà*	理发
half	*èrfēn zhīyī (yíbàn)*	二分之一（一半）
half an hour	*bàngè xiǎoshí*	半个小时
half past three	*sān diǎn bàn*	三点半

English	*Pinyin*	Chinese
ham	*huǒtuǐ*	火腿
hand	*shǒu*	手
handkerchief	*shǒujuàn*	手绢
hanger	*yījià*	衣架
happy	*gāoxìng*	高兴
hard	*yìng*	硬
hard seat	*yìngzuò*	硬座
hard sleeper	*yìngwò*	硬卧
have	*yǒu*	有
have a rest	*xiūxi*	休息
have one's blood tested	*yànxiě*	验血
he	*tā*	他
head	*tóu*	头
headache	*tóu tòng*	头痛
health certificate	*jiànkāng zhèngmíngshū*	健康证明书
hear	*tīngjian*	听见
heart	*xīnzàng*	心脏
heart disease	*xīnzàngbìng*	心脏病
heating	*nuǎnqì*	暖气
heavy	*zhòng*	重
heavy rain	*dàyǔ*	大雨

English	*Pinyin*	Chinese
hectare (unit of measure)	*gōngqǐng*	公顷
heel	*jiǎogēn*	脚跟
hello	*nǐhǎo*	你好
help	*bāngzhù*	帮助
hepatitis	*gānyán*	肝炎
her	*tāde*	她的
here	*zhèlǐ, zhèr*	这里，这儿
high	*gāo*	高
high quality	*gāo zhìliàng*	高质量
hill	*xiǎoshān*	小山
hip	*túnbù*	臀部
his	*tāde*	他的
Hong Kong currency	*gǎngbì*	港币
horse	*mǎ*	马
hospital	*yīyuàn*	医院
(be) hospitalized	*zhùyuàn*	住院
hot	*rède*	热的
hot water	*rèshuǐ*	热水
hot water bottle	*rèshuǐdài*	热水袋
hotel	*lǚguǎn, fàndiàn*	旅馆，饭店
hour	*xiǎoshí*	小时

English	*Pinyin*	Chinese
how	*zěnmeyàng*	怎么样
how big	*duō dà*	多大
how far	*duōyuǎn*	多远
how long	*duōjiǔ, duōcháng*	多久，多长
how much	*duōshǎo*	多少
humid	*mènrè*	闷热
hungry	*è*	饿
hurry	*kuài yìdiǎn*	快一点
husband	*zhàngfū*	丈夫
I	*wǒ*	我
iced beer	*bīngzhèn píjiǔ*	冰镇啤酒
import	*jìnkǒu*	进口
in the afternoon	*xiàwǔ*	下午
in the evening	*wǎnshàng*	晚上
in the morning	*shàngwǔ*	上午
inch	*yīngcùn*	英寸
income	*shōurù*	收入
infection	*gǎnrǎn*	感染
injection	*dǎzhēn*	打针
injection room	*zhùshèshì*	注射室
ink	*mòshuǐ*	墨水

English	*Pinyin*	Chinese
insect	*kūnchóng, chóngzi*	昆虫，虫子
inside	*lǐbiān*	里边
institute	*xuéyuàn*	学院
insurance	*bǎoxiǎn*	保险
interest rate	*lìlǜ*	利率
(be) interested in	*duì…gǎn xìngqù*	对 … 感兴趣
interesting	*yǒu yìsi*	有意思
intermission	*xiūxi*	休息
international call	*guójì chángtú*	国际长途
Int'l Women's Day (March 8)	*sān bā fùnǚjié*	三八妇女节
interpreter	*fānyì*	翻译
intestines	*chángzi*	肠子
invitational tournament	*yāoqǐngsài*	邀请赛
iodine	*diǎnjiǔ*	碘酒
island	*dǎo*	岛
Italian	*Yìdàlì rén*	意大利人
itch	*yǎng*	痒
itinerary	*lǚxíng lùxiàn*	旅行路线
ivory	*xiàngyá*	象牙
jade	*yù*	玉

English	Pinyin	Chinese
jadestone	*yùshí*	玉石
jam (food)	*guǒjiàng*	果酱
January	*yíyuè*	一月
Japanese (people)	*Rìběn rén*	日本人
Japanese (language)	*Rìwén*	日文
Japanese yen	*rì yuán*	日元
jasmine tea	*mòlìhuāchá*	茉莉花茶
jewel case	*shǒushì hé*	首饰盒
jewelry	*zhūbǎo*	珠宝
jiao (=1/10 *yuan* or 10 *fen*)	*jiǎo, máo*	角，毛
joint venture	*hézī qǐyè*	合资企业
journalist	*jìzhě*	记者
juice	*shuǐguǒzhī*	水果汁
July	*qīyuè*	七月
June	*liùyuè*	六月
keep out	*qiè wù rùnèi*	切勿入内
key	*yàoshi*	钥匙
kidney	*shèn*	肾
kidney beans	*yāodòu*	腰豆
kidskin	*xiǎo shānyángpí*	小山羊皮
kilogram	*gōngjīn*	公斤

English	*Pinyin*	Chinese
kilometer	*gōnglǐ*	公里
kindergarten	*yòu'éryuán*	幼儿园
knee	*xī*	膝
knife	*dāozi*	刀子
know	*zhīdào*	知道
Labor Day (May 1)	*wǔyī láodòng jié*	五一劳动节
laboratory	*huàyànshì*	化验室
lacquerware	*qīqì*	漆器
ladies' room	*nǚcèsuǒ*	女厕所
lake	*hú*	湖
land (v)	*jiàngluò*	降落
landscape	*fēngjǐng*	风景
large bills	*dà'é chāopiào*	大额钞票
last	*hòu*	后
last night	*zuówǎn*	昨晚
last stop	*zhōngdiǎnzhàn*	终点站
late	*wǎn*	晚
laundry	*xǐyīdiàn*	洗衣店
lawyer	*lǜshī*	律师
lean (thin)	*shòude*	瘦的
learn	*xué*	学

English	*Pinyin*	Chinese
leather	*pí, pízi*	皮，皮子
leather gloves	*píshǒutào*	皮手套
leather shoes	*pí xié*	皮鞋
leave	*líkāi*	离开
leave a message	*liúyán*	留言
left	*zuǒ*	左
leg	*tuǐ*	腿
lemon	*níngméng*	柠檬
lens	*jìngtóu*	镜头
let	*ràng*	让
letter	*xìn*	信
letter of credit	*xìnyòng zhèng*	信用证
letter of introduction	*jièshàoxìn*	介绍信
lettuce	*shēngcài*	生菜
librarian	*túshūguǎn guǎnlǐyuán*	图书馆管理员
library	*túshūguǎn*	图书馆
light (lamp)	*dēng*	灯
light (weight)	*qīng*	轻
light (color)	*qiǎn, dàn*	浅，淡
lighter	*dǎhuǒjī*	打火机
like	*xǐhuān*	喜欢

English	*Pinyin*	Chinese
lips	*zuǐchún*	嘴唇
lipstick	*kǒuhóng*	口红
listen	*tīng*	听
litchi (lichee-fruit)	*lìzhī*	荔枝
liver	*gān*	肝
loan	*dàikuǎn*	贷款
lobby	*qiántīng*	前厅
lobster	*lóngxiā*	龙虾
local map	*dāngdì dìtú*	当地地图
local opera	*dìfāngxì*	地方戏
local specialties	*tèchǎn*	特产
long	*cháng*	长
long distance	*chángtú*	长途
long distance call	*chángtú diànhuà*	长途电话
longan (fruit)	*lóngyǎn*	龙眼
look	*kàn*	看
look for	*xúnzhǎo*	寻找
loose	*sōng*	松
lose (defeat)	*shū*	输
lose (mislay)	*diū*	丢
loss	*sǔnshī*	损失

English	*Pinyin*	Chinese
(be) lost	*mílù le*	迷路了
lotus root	*ǒu*	藕
louder	*dàshēng yìdiǎn*	大声一点
lounge	*xiūxishì*	休息室
low	*dī*	低
lower	*jiàngdī*	降低
luggage check	*xínglǐpiào*	行李票
lunch	*wǔfàn*	午饭
lungs	*fèibù*	肺部
machine	*jīqì*	机器
mackeral	*qīngyú*	鲭鱼
magic show	*móshù*	魔术
mail box	*yóuxiāng*	邮箱
main role	*zhǔjué*	主角
main street	*dàjiē*	大街
make a call	*dǎ diànhuà*	打电话
make an exception	*tōngróng yíxià*	通融一下
malaria	*nüèji*	疟疾
mango	*mángguǒ*	芒果
many	*hěnduō*	很多
March	*sānyuè*	三月

English	*Pinyin*	Chinese
market	*shìchǎng*	市场
martial arts	*wǔshù*	武术
matches	*huǒchái*	火柴
matter	*wèntí, shìqing*	问题，事情
may	*kěyǐ*	可以
May	*wǔyuè*	五月
meat	*ròu*	肉
mecurochrome	*hónggǒng*	红汞
medical school	*yīxuéyuàn*	医学院
medical treatment	*zhìliáo*	治疗
medicine	*yào*	药
medicine for sea-sickness	*zhǐyūnyào*	止晕药
meet	*rènshì*	认识
meet (one's) requirement	*mǎnzú yāoqiú*	满足要求
men's room	*náncèsuǒ*	男厕所
menu	*càidān*	菜单
meter	*mǐ*	米
middle school	*zhōngxué*	中学
mile	*yīnglǐ*	英里
millimeter	*háomǐ*	毫米
mine (*pron.*)	*wǒde*	我的

English	*Pinyin*	Chinese
minerals	*kuàngchǎnpǐn*	矿产品
mineral water	*kuàngquánshuǐ*	矿泉水
mini bus	*miànbāo chē*	面包车
mink	*shuǐdiāo*	水貂
minute	*fēn*	分
mirror	*jìngzi*	镜子
Miss	*xǐaojiě*	小姐
model (sample)	*yàngpǐn*	样品
modern drama	*huàjù*	话剧
monastery	*sìyuàn*	寺院
Monday	*xīngqīyī*	星期一
money	*qián*	钱
month	*yuè*	月
mouth	*zuǐ*	嘴
murals	*bìhuà*	壁画
museum	*bówùguǎn*	博物馆
mushrooms	*dōnggū*	冬菇
music	*yīnyuè*	音乐
musician	*yīnyuèjiā*	音乐家
mutton	*yángròu*	羊肉
my	*wǒde*	我的

English	*Pinyin*	Chinese
name	*míngzi*	名字
napkin	*cānjīn*	餐巾
narrow	*zhǎi*	窄
National Day (October 1)	*Guóqìngjié*	国庆节
near	*jìn*	近
neck	*bózi*	脖子
need	*xūyào*	需要
needle and thread	*zhēn xiàn*	针线
negotiate	*tánpàn*	谈判
nerves	*shénjīng*	神经
new	*xīn*	新
New Year picture	*nián huà*	年画
newsreel	*xīnwén piàn*	新闻片
next year	*míngnián*	明年
night cream	*wǎn shuāng*	晚霜
nine	*jiǔ*	九
nine hundred	*jiǔbǎi*	九百
nineteen	*shíjiǔ*	十九
ninety	*jiǔshí*	九十
ninth	*dìjiǔ*	第九
no	*búshì, búduì bùhǎo*	不是，不对，不好

English	*Pinyin*	Chinese
no admittance	*mò rù*	莫入
no entrance	*jìnzhǐ rùnèi*	禁止入内
no more	*gòu le*	够了
no photos allowed	*jìnzhǐ zhàoxiàng*	禁止照相
no smoking	*jìnzhǐ xīyān*	禁止吸烟
no swimming	*jìnzhǐ yóuyǒng*	禁止游泳
no use	*bù qǐ zuòyòng*	不起作用
noisy	*chǎonào*	吵闹
noodles	*miàntiáo*	面条
noodles in soup	*tāngmiàn*	汤面
north	*běi*	北
nose	*bízi*	鼻子
nothing	*méiyǒu shénme*	没有什么
notice	*tōngzhīdān*	通知单
November	*shíyīyuè*	十一月
now	*xiànzài*	现在
number	*hàomǎ*	号码
nurse	*hùshi*	护士
o'clock	*diǎnzhōng*	点钟
October	*shíyuè*	十月
O.K.	*hǎo, kěyǐ*	好，可以

English	*Pinyin*	Chinese
old (age)	*lǎo*	老
old (past)	*jiù*	旧
on vacation	*dùjià*	度假
on schedule	*zhǔndiǎn*	准点
one	*yī*	一
one half	*èrfēn zhīyī*	二分之一
one hundred	*yìbǎi*	一百
one hundred million	*yíyì*	一亿
one hundred thousand	*shíwàn*	十万
one quarter	*sìfēn zhīyī*	四分之一
one spoonful	*yī sháo*	一勺
one tablet	*yí piàn*	一片
one third	*sānfēn zhīyī*	三分之一
one thousand	*yìqīan*	一千
one yuan fifty-five fen	*yí kuài wǔmáo wǔ*	一块五毛五
open	*dǎkāi*	打开
open an account	*kāilì zhànghù*	开立帐户
opera	*gējù*	歌剧
opera singer	*gējù yǎnyuán*	歌剧演员
operator	*zǒngjī*	总机
or	*háishi, huòzhě*	还是，或者

English	*Pinyin*	Chinese
orange (fruit)	*júzi*	橘子
orange (color)	*chéngsè*	橙色
order dishes in a restaurant	*diǎncài*	点菜
ordinary	*zhèngcháng*	正常
original painting	*yuánhuà*	原画
others	*biéde*	别的
otter	*shuǐtǎ*	水獭
ounce	*àngsī*	盎司
output	*chǎnliàng*	产量
outside	*wàibiān*	外边
overweight	*chāozhòng*	超重
pagoda	*tǎ*	塔
pain	*téng*	疼
painting in Chinese ink	*shuǐmòhuà*	水墨画
painting shop	*shūhuàdiàn*	书画店
paintings	*huà*	画
panda	*xióngmāo*	熊猫
papercut	*jiǎnzhǐ*	剪纸
paragoric	*zhǐténgjì*	止疼剂
parcel	*bāoguǒ*	包裹
park (*n*)	*gōngyuán*	公园

English	*Pinyin*	Chinese
parts	*língjiàn*	零件
passenger office	*kèyùnshì*	客运室
passport	*hùzhào*	护照
passport control	*jiǎnyàn hùzhào*	检验护照
paste (glue)	*jiànghu*	浆糊
pavilion	*tíng*	亭
pay	*fù kuǎn*	付款
peach	*táozi*	桃子
peanuts	*huāshēng*	花生
pear	*lízi*	梨子
peas	*wāndòu*	豌豆
peasant	*nóngmín*	农民
peculiar	*qíguài*	奇怪
pedestrian crossing	*rénxíng héngdào*	人行横道
Peking Duck	*Běijīng kǎoyā*	北京烤鸭
Peking Opera	*jīngjù*	京剧
pension	*tuìxiūjīn*	退休金
People's Bank of China	*Zhōngguó Rénmín Yínháng*	中国人民银行
pepper oil	*làjiāo yóu*	辣椒油
per	*měi*	每
percent	*bǎi fēnzhī*	百分之

English	*Pinyin*	Chinese
performance	*yǎnchū*	演出
perfume	*xiāngshuǐ*	香水
perhaps	*kěnéng*	可能
persimmon	*shìzi*	柿子
personal	*zìjǐ, gèrén*	自己，个人
pharmacy	*yàofáng*	药房
phone	*diànhuà*	电话
photographer	*shèyǐngshī*	摄影师
pig	*zhū*	猪
pill	*yàowán*	药丸
pillow	*zhěntou*	枕头
pilot's bridge	*jiàshǐtái*	驾驶台
pineapple	*bōluó*	菠萝
pink	*fěnhóng (de)*	粉红（的）
place	*dìfāng*	地方
place an order	*dìnghuò*	订货
plan	*jìhuà*	计划
plane ticket	*fēijīpiào*	飞机票
plate	*pánzi*	盘子
platform	*zhàntái*	站台
platform ticket	*zhàntáipiào*	站台票

English	*Pinyin*	Chinese
play (recreation)	*xì*	戏
play (perform)	*bànyǎn*	扮演
please	*qǐng*	请
plug	*sāizi*	塞子
plums	*lǐzi*	李子
pneumonia	*fèiyán*	肺炎
policy	*zhèngcè*	政策
poor	*qióng*	穷
porcelain	*cíqì*	瓷器
porridge	*zhōu*	粥
port (harbor)	*gǎngkǒu*	港口
post office	*yóujú*	邮局
postage due	*qiàn yóuzī*	欠邮资
postcards	*míngxìnpiàn*	明信片
postman	*yóudìyuán*	邮递员
postmark	*yóuchuō*	邮戳
pottery	*táoqì*	陶器
pound	*bàng*	镑
pounds sterling	*yīngbàng*	英镑
prawn	*dàxiā*	大虾
prescription	*yàofāng*	药方

English	*Pinyin*	Chinese
price	*jiàqián*	价钱
price list	*jiàgédān*	价格单
primary school	*xiǎoxué*	小学
product	*chǎnpǐn*	产品
profession	*zhíyè*	职业
professor	*jiàoshòu*	教授
profit	*lìrùn*	利润
program	*jiémùdān*	节目单
provide	*tígòng*	提供
prunes (plums)	*méizi*	梅子
public bus	*gōnggòng qìchē*	公共汽车
publications	*shūkān*	书刊
pulse	*màibó*	脉博
puppet theater	*mù'ǒuxì*	木偶戏
pure wool	*chún yángmáo*	纯羊毛
purple	*zǐsè (de)*	紫色（的）
Qingming Festival (April 5)	*qīngmíng jié*	清明节
quarter of an hour	*yíkè zhōng*	一刻钟
quarter to twelve	*chà yíkè shíèrdiǎn*	差一刻十二点
quick	*kuài*	快
quiet	*ānjìng*	安静

English	Pinyin	Chinese
quilt	*bèizi*	被子
quoted price	*bàojià*	报价
rabbit	*tùzi*	兔子
radio	*shōuyīnjī*	收音机
rain	*yǔ, xiàyǔ*	雨，下雨
rainshoes	*yǔxié*	雨鞋
raisins	*pútáogān*	葡萄干
rate	*jiàgé*	价格
razor blades	*tìdāo dāopiàn*	剃刀刀片
receipt	*shōujù*	收据
record (gramaphone)	*chàngpiān*	唱片
record (sound)	*lùyīn*	录音
recorder	*lùyīnjī*	录音机
red	*hóng (de)*	红（的）
reduce	*jiàngdī*	降低
referee	*cáipànyuán*	裁判员
registered mail	*guàhàoxìn*	挂号信
registration desk	*dēngjì tái*	登记台
registration office	*guàhaòshì*	挂号室
remittance	*huìkuǎn*	汇款
rent	*zū, zūjīn*	租，租金

English	*Pinyin*	Chinese
researcher	*yánjiūyuán*	研究员
reservation	*yùdìng*	预订
reserved	*bǎoliú*	保留
rest	*xiūxi*	休息
rest room	*cèsuǒ*	厕所
restaurant	*fànguǎn*	饭馆
rheumatism	*fēngshī*	风湿
rice	*dàozi, mǐfàn*	稻子，米饭
rich	*fù*	富
right (direction)	*yòu*	右
right (correct)	*duì*	对
ring	*jièzhi*	戒指
river	*hé*	河
roast	*kǎo*	烤
room number	*fánghào*	房号
rosebush	*méiguì shù*	玫瑰树
runny nose	*liú bítì*	流鼻涕
rural enterprise	*xiāngzhèn qǐyè*	乡镇企业
sable	*hēidiāo, báidiāo*	黑貂，白貂
sad	*bù gāoxìng*	不高兴
safe	*ānquán*	安全

English	Pinyin	Chinese
sail	*hángxíng*	航行
sailing schedule	*chuánqībiǎo*	船期表
sailor	*shuǐshǒu*	水手
sales	*chūshòu*	出售
salty	*xiánde*	咸的
sandals	*liángxié*	凉鞋
satin	*duànzi*	缎子
Saturday	*xīngqīliù*	星期六
saute	*chǎo*	炒
scarf	*wéijīn*	围巾
scenic site	*fēngjǐng diǎn*	风景点
scientist	*kēxuéjiā*	科学家
scrambled eggs	*chǎojīdàn*	炒鸡蛋
screen	*yínmù*	银幕
sealed	*fēngkǒu*	封口
seats	*zuòwèi*	座位
second (time)	*miǎo*	秒
second (number)	*dì'èr*	第二
second-class (cabin)	*èrděng (cāng)*	二等（舱）
secretary	*mìshū*	秘书
see	*kàn*	看

English	Pinyin	Chinese
sell	*mài, xiāoshòu*	卖，销售
send	*jì*	寄
send a letter	*jìxìn*	寄信
send a telegram	*pāi diànbào*	拍电报
send back	*tuìhuí*	退回
sender	*fāxìn rén*	发信人
September	*jiǔyuè*	九月
serious	*yánzhòng*	严重
service counter	*fúwùbù*	服务部
service desk	*fúwùtái*	服务台
sesame oil	*xiāngyóu*	香油
seven	*qī*	七
seven hundred	*qībǎi*	七百
seventeen	*shíqī*	十七
seventh	*dìqī*	第七
seventy	*qīshí*	七十
several	*jǐgè*	几个
shallow	*qiǎn*	浅
shampoo	*xǐfǎgāo, xǐfǎjì*	洗发膏，洗发剂
shave	*guāliǎn*	刮脸
she	*tā*	她

English	*Pinyin*	Chinese
sheet	*chuángdān*	床单
ship (transport)	*zhuāngyùn*	装运
ship (boat)	*chúan*	船
shirt	*nán chènshān*	男衬衫
shoes	*xié*	鞋
shop	*xiǎomàibù*	小卖部
shopping	*mǎi dōngxī*	买东西
shopping area	*shāngyè qū*	商业区
short	*duǎn, ǎi*	短，矮
shoulder	*jiān*	肩
show (me)	*gěi wǒ kànkàn*	给我看看
shrimp	*xiā*	虾
shrimp dumplings	*xiā jiǎo*	虾饺
shut	*guān*	关
side street	*hútòng*	胡同
sidewalk	*biàndào*	便道
sights of interest	*míngshèng*	名胜
sign, signature	*qiānmíng*	签名
signet (seal)	*yìnzhāng*	印章
simple	*jiǎndān*	简单
single room	*dānrén fángjiān*	单人房间

English	Pinyin	Chinese
Sino-foreign joint venture	*Zhōngwài hézī*	中外合资
sit	*zuò*	坐
six	*liù*	六
six hundred	*liùbǎi*	六百
sixteen	*shíliù*	十六
sixth	*dìliù*	第六
sixty	*liùshí*	六十
skin	*pí, pífū*	皮，皮肤
skirt	*qúnzi*	裙子
sleep	*shuìjiào*	睡觉
sleeping pills	*ānmián yào*	安眠药
slippers	*tuōxié*	拖鞋
slow	*màn*	慢
slower, slowly	*màn yìdiǎn*	慢一点
small	*xiǎo*	小
small bills	*xiǎo'é chāopiào*	小额钞票
small change	*língqián*	零钱
smaller	*xiǎo yìdiǎn*	小一点
small steamed pork buns	*xiǎolóngbāo*	小笼包
smart	*cōngming*	聪明
snack	*kuàicān*	快餐

English	*Pinyin*	Chinese
snack counter	*xiǎomàibù*	小卖部
snow	*xuě, xiàxuě*	雪，下雪
soap	*féizào*	肥皂
soccer	*zú qiú*	足球
soft	*ruǎn*	软
soft drinks	*qìshuǐ*	汽水
soft sleeper	*ruǎnwò*	软卧
sold out	*shòu wán*	售完
song and dance	*gēwǔ*	歌舞
soon	*mǎshàng*	马上
sore throat	*hóulóng téng*	喉咙疼
soup	*tāng*	汤
sour	*suānde*	酸的
south	*nán*	南
souvenir	*jìniànpǐn*	纪念品
souvenir shop	*jìniànpǐn shāngdiàn*	纪念品商店
soy sauce	*jiàngyóu*	酱油
Spanish (language)	*Xībānyáwén*	西班牙文
spare parts	*bèijiàn*	备件
speak	*shuō*	说
special delivery	*zhuāndì xìn*	专递信

English	Pinyin	Chinese
specialty (food)	*tèshū fēngwèi cài*	特殊风味菜
spicy	*là de*	辣的
spinach	*bōcài*	菠菜
spine	*jǐgǔ, jǐliáng*	脊骨，脊梁
spoon	*sháozi*	勺子
sports	*tǐyù*	体育
spring (the season)	*chūntiān*	春天
spring rolls	*chūnjuǎn*	春卷
square	*guǎngchǎng*	广场
stairs	*lóutī*	楼梯
stamp	*yóupiào*	邮票
stamp catalog	*yóupiào mùlù*	邮票目录
state-run factory	*guó yíng gōngchǎng*	国营工厂
stationary	*xìnzhǐ*	信纸
stay	*tíngliú, zhù*	停留，住
steam	*qīngzhēng*	清蒸
steamed buns	*mántou*	馒头
steamed dumpling	*zhēngjiǎo*	蒸饺
steamed pork dumpling	*shāomài*	烧麦
steamed roast pork buns	*chá shāo bāo*	叉烧包
steamed rolls	*huājuǎn*	花卷

English	*Pinyin*	Chinese
steamer, steam boat	*lúnchuán*	轮船
stir-fry	*chǎo*	炒
stockings	*chángtǒngwà*	长统袜
stomach	*wèi*	胃
stomach-ache	*wèi tòng*	胃痛
stone rubbings	*tuòbēi*	拓碑
stop	*tíng*	停
storm	*bàofēngyǔ*	暴风雨
straight ahead	*yìzhí zǒu*	一直走
strawberries	*cǎoméi*	草莓
street	*jiēdào*	街道
strong	*zhuàng*	壮
student	*xuéshēng*	学生
study	*xué*	学
stupid	*bèn*	笨
sturgeon	*huángyú*	黄鱼
style	*kuǎnshì*	款式
suggest	*jiànyì*	建议
suit	*(yítào) yīfu*	（一套）衣服
suitcase	*xiāngzi*	箱子
suite	*tàojiān*	套间

English	*Pinyin*	Chinese
summer	*xiàtiān*	夏天
Sunday	*xīngqīrì*	星期日
sunny	*yǒu tàiyáng*	有太阳
surface mail	*píng yóu*	平邮
surgeon	*wàikē yīshēng*	外科医生
surgery	*shǒushù*	手术
sweater	*máoyī*	毛衣
sweet	*tiánde*	甜的
sweet bean buns	*dòushābāo*	豆沙包
sweet rice with meat stuffing in lotus leaves	*nuòmǐ zòngzi*	糯米粽子
Swiss francs	*Ruìshì fǎláng*	瑞士法郎
symphonic music	*jiāoxiǎngyuè*	交响乐
table cloth	*zhuōbù*	桌布
table tennis	*pīngpāngqiú*	乒乓球
take medicine	*fúyào*	服药
take off	*qǐfēi*	起飞
take one's temperature	*liáng tǐwēn*	量体温
tall	*gāo*	高
tangerine	*júzi*	橘子
tapestry	*guàtǎn*	挂毯

English	*Pinyin*	Chinese
taxi	*chūzūchē*	出租车
taxi driver	*sījī*	司机
tea	*chá*	茶
tea service	*chájù*	茶具
teacher	*lǎoshī*	老师
teacher's college	*shīfàn dàxué*	师范大学
teacup	*chábēi*	茶杯
team	*duì*	队
teapot	*cháhú*	茶壶
technician	*jìshùyuán*	技术员
telegram	*diànbào*	电报
telephone	*diànhuà*	电话
telephone number	*diànhuà hàomǎ*	电话号码
telex	*diànchuán*	电传
television	*diànshìjī*	电视机
tell	*gàosù*	告诉
temperature	*wēndù*	温度
temple	*miào*	庙
ten	*shí*	十
ten *fen*=one *jiao* (*mao*)	*shífēn=yīmáo*	十分 = 一毛
ten *jiao* (*mao*)=one *yuan*	*shímáo=yīyuán*	十毛 = 一元

English	Pinyin	Chinese
ten thousand	*yíwàn*	一万
tenth	*dìshí*	第十
terms of payment	*fùkuǎn tiáojiàn*	付款条件
thank, thanks	*xièxiè*	谢谢
theater	*jùchǎng*	剧场
there	*nàli, nàr*	那里，那儿
thermometer	*tǐwēnbiǎo*	体温表
they	*tāmén*	他们
thick	*hòu*	厚
thin	*bó*	薄
third	*dìsān*	第三
third class (cabin)	*sānděng (cāng)*	三等（舱）
thirteen	*shísán*	十三
thirty	*sānshí*	三十
this	*zhè*	这
this month	*zhège yuè*	这个月
this week	*zhège xīngqī*	这个星期
this year	*jīn nián*	今年
three	*sān*	三
three hundred	*sānbǎi*	三百
three o'clock	*sāndiǎn zhōng*	三点钟

English	*Pinyin*	Chinese
three quarters	*sìfēn zhīsān*	四分之三
three thirty	*sāndiǎn sānshífēn*	三点三十分
three times a day	*měitiān sān cì*	每天三次
throat	*hóulóng*	喉咙
thunder	*léi*	雷
Thursday	*xīngqīsì*	星期四
ticket	*piào*	票
ticket office	*shòupiàochù*	售票处
ticket seller	*shòupiàoyuán*	售票员
tight	*jǐn*	紧
time	*shíhou*	时候
(be, get) tired	*lèi le*	累了
toast	*kǎomiànbāo*	烤面包
today	*jīntiān*	今天
toe	*jiǎozhǐ*	脚趾
toilet paper	*wèishēngzhǐ*	卫生纸
toiletries	*huàzhuāng yòngpǐn*	化妆用品
tomatoes	*xīhóngshì*	西红柿
tomorrow	*míngtiān*	明天
tonsils	*biǎntáoxiàn*	扁桃腺
too	*tài*	太

English	*Pinyin*	Chinese
tooth	*yáchǐ*	牙齿
tooth-ache	*yá tòng*	牙痛
toothbrush	*yá shuā*	牙刷
toothpaste	*yágāo*	牙膏
toothpicks	*yáqiān*	牙签
toward	*xiàng*	向
towel	*máojīn*	毛巾
trade	*màoyì*	贸易
trade fair	*jiāoyìhuì*	交易会
trade union	*gōnghuì*	工会
traffic lights	*hónglùdēng*	红绿灯
train	*huǒchē*	火车
train schedule	*huǒchē shíkèbiǎo*	火车时刻表
train station	*huǒchēzhàn*	火车站
traquilizer	*āndìng yào*	安定药
translate	*fānyì*	翻译
travel	*lǚxíng*	旅行
travelers's check	*lǚxíng zhīpiào*	旅行支票
traveling bag	*lǚxíngbǎo*	旅行包
tree	*shù*	树
tripod	*sānjiǎojià*	三脚架

English	*Pinyin*	Chinese
trouble	*máfan*	麻烦
true	*zhēn*	真
try	*shì yī shì*	试一试
tuberculosis	*fèijiéhé*	肺结核
Tuesday	*xīngqī'èr*	星期二
turn off (the light)	*guān (dēng)*	关（灯）
turn on (the light)	*kāi (dēng)*	开（灯）
turnip cake	*luóbo gāo*	萝卜糕
TV program	*diànshì jiémù*	电视节目
twelve	*shí'èr*	十二
twenty	*èrshí*	二十
twenty-five	*èrshíwǔ*	二十五
twenty-one	*èrshíyī*	二十一
two	*èr*	二
two hundred	*èrbǎi*	二百
typhoon	*táifēng*	台风
ugly	*chǒu*	丑
ulcer	*kuìyáng*	溃疡
ultrasonic wave	*chāoshēngbō*	超声波
under	*xiàbiān*	下边
underground station	*dìtiě zhàn*	地铁站

English	*Pinyin*	Chinese
underpants	*nèikù*	内裤
undershirt	*neìyī*	内衣
understand	*dǒng*	懂
university	*dàxué*	大学
upstairs	*lóushàng*	楼上
urgent telegram	*jiājídiànbào*	加急电报
urine	*niào*	尿
U.S. dollars	*měiyuán*	美元
use	*shǐyòng*	使用
usual medicine	*chángyòngyào*	常用药
usual practice	*xíguàn zuòfǎ*	习惯作法
vase	*huāpíng*	花瓶
vaseline	*fánshìlín*	凡士林
vegetarian	*sùshízhě*	素食者
vein	*xuèguǎn, jìngmài*	血管，静脉
very	*hěn*	很
village fair (free market)	*zìyóu shìchǎng*	自由市场
vinegar	*cù*	醋
visa	*qiānzhèng*	签证
visit	*fǎngwèn*	访问
vitamin	*wéishēngsù*	维生素

English	*Pinyin*	Chinese
volleyball	*páiqiú*	排球
vomiting	*ǒutù*	呕吐
wage	*gōngzī*	工资
wait for	*děng*	等
waiter	*fúwùyuán*	服务员
waiting room (ship)	*hòuchuánshì*	侯船室
waiting room (airport)	*hòujī shì*	侯机室
walk	*zǒulù*	走路
walnuts	*hétao*	核桃
want	*yào*	要
wash	*xǐ*	洗
watch	*biǎo*	表
water	*shuǐ*	水
water buffalo	*shuǐniú*	水牛
water-color painting	*shuǐcǎihuà*	水彩画
watermelon	*xīguā*	西瓜
we	*wǒmen*	我们
weak	*ruò*	弱
weather	*tiānqì*	天气
weather forecast	*tiānqì yùbào*	天气预报
Wednesday	*xīngqīsān*	星期三

English	*Pinyin*	Chinese
week	*xīngqī*	星期
weekend	*zhōumò*	周末
welcome	*huānyíng*	欢迎
west	*xī*	西
western food	*xīcān*	西餐
western medicine	*xīyào*	西药
western restaurant	*xīcānguǎn*	西餐馆
wet	*shī*	湿
what	*shénme*	什么
wheat	*màizi*	麦子
when	*shénme shíhou*	什么时候
where	*nǎlǐ, nǎr*	哪里，哪儿
which	*nǎgè*	哪个
whiskey	*wēishìjì*	威士忌
white	*bái (de)*	白（的）
who	*shéi*	谁
whole (entire)	*zhěnggè*	整个
why	*wèishénme*	为什么
wide	*kuān*	宽
wife	*tàitai*	太太
win	*yíng*	赢

English	Pinyin	Chinese
windy	*yǒu fēng*	有风
wine	*pútaojiǔ*	葡萄酒
winter	*dōngtiān*	冬天
withdraw money	*qǔ qián*	取钱
wonderful	*hǎojíle*	好极了
wontons	*húntun*	馄饨
wood	*mù*	木
wood block printing	*mùbǎn shuǐyìn huà*	木版水印画
word	*zì*	字
worker	*gōngrén*	工人
would like	*xiǎng*	想
wrist	*shǒuwàn*	手腕
write	*xiě*	写
writer	*zuòjiā*	作家
wrong	*cuòde*	错的
x-ray	*tòushì*	透视
year	*nián*	年
yellow	*huáng (de)*	黄（的）
yes	*shìde, duìde, hǎode*	是的，对的，好的
yesterday	*zuótiān*	昨天
yogurt	*suānnǎi*	酸奶

English	*Pinyin*	Chinese
you	*nǐ, nín*	你，您
you (pl.)	*nǐmen*	你们
young	*niánqīng*	年轻
your, yours	*nǐde*	你的
yuan	*yuán, kuài*	元，块
zero	*líng*	零
zip code	*yóuzhèng biānmǎ*	邮政编码
zoo	*dòngwùyuán*	动物园